Contemporary Poetry
of North Carolina

Contemporary Poetry of North Carolina

edited by **GUY OWEN** and **MARY C. WILLIAMS**

JOHN F. BLAIR, Publisher
Winston-Salem, North Carolina

Copyright © 1977 by Guy Owen and Mary C. Williams
Library of Congress Catalog Card Number: 77–20809
ISBN 0–910244–98–7
All rights reserved
Printed in the United States of America
by Heritage Printers, Inc.
Charlotte, North Carolina

Library of Congress Cataloging in Publication Data
Main entry under title:

Contemporary poetry of North Carolina.

  Bibliography: p.
  1. American poetry—North Carolina. 2. American
poetry—20th century. I. Owen, Guy, 1925–
II. Williams, Mary C., 1923–
PS558.N8C64   811'.5'408   77–20809
ISBN 0–910244–98–77

To RICHARD WALSER, for a lifetime of devotion to North Carolina letters

Acknowledgments

THE EDITORS are grateful to the following authors and publishers for permission to reprint poems from the works listed below:

The American Scholar for "Insomnia" by Kathryn Stripling, reprinted from Vol. 43, No. 4, Autumn, 1974, copyright © 1974 by the United Chapters of Phi Beta Kappa.

Appalachian Consortium Press for "Cherry Tree" from *Mountain Measure* by Francis Pledger Hulme.

Atheneum Publishers for "The Woman at the Washington Zoo" from the book of the same name by Randall Jarrell, copyright © 1960 by Randall Jarrell, reprinted by permission of Atheneum Publishers; "The Radio Astronomer," "Going Nowhere Alone at Night," and "Planet Eight," from *Selected Poems*, copyright © 1966, 1971, 1974 by Robert Watson. "The Radio Astronomer" and "Planet Eight" were included in Mr. Watson's *Christmas in Las Vegas*, and "Going Nowhere Alone at Night" in his *Advantages of Dark*, reprinted by permission of Atheneum Publishers.

John F. Blair, Publisher, for "Contrasts" from *Step Carefully in Night Grass* by Susan Bartels; "The Philadelphia Airport" from *The Casketmaker* by Ronald H. Bayes; "At Nobska" and "A Mobile" from *The Chastening of Narcissus* by Harold Grier McCurdy; "My Father's Curse" from *The White Stallion and Other Poems* by Guy Owen; " 'The Prophet' " and "Flannery O'Connor" from *The Tree in the Far Pasture* by Sam Ragan.

Broadside Press for "When I Know the Power of My Black Hand" from the book of the same name, copyright © 1974 by Lance Jeffers.

Coraddi for "The Last Straw" by James Bardon.

Crucible for "Moving North" by Ann Deagon.

The Curveship Press for "Lost Colony" from *Hearts and Gizzards* by Marvin Weaver.

Charles Edward Eaton for "The Goose" from *On the Edge of the Knife*, Abelard-Schuman; "Girl Raking Hay" and "The Image on the Knee" from *The Man in the Green Chair*, A. S. Barnes.

Farrar, Straus & Giroux, Inc., for "90 North," copyright 1941 by Randall Jarrell, renewed © 1968 by Mrs. Randall Jarrell, and "A Pilot from the Carrier," copyright 1941 by Randall Jarrell, renewed © 1973 by Mary von Schrader Jarrell, from *The Complete Poems* by Randall Jarrell, reprinted with the permission of Farrar, Straus & Giroux, Inc.

The Georgia Review for "At Nobska" by Harold Grier McCurdy, Winter, 1959, issue.

International Review for "Tod und das Weib" by Ann Deagon.

Jackpine Press for "Balancing on Stones" from the book of the same name by Emily Wilson.

Louisiana State University Press for "The Farm" and "Skin Flick" from *The World Between the Eyes* by Fred Chappell, copyright © 1971; "Cleaning the Well" from *River* by Fred Chappell, copyright © 1975; "Walking Out," "Identity," and "Southbound" from *Walking Out* by Betty Adcock, copyright © 1975.

Norman Macleod for "Thanksgiving Before November" from *The Selected Poems of Norman Macleod*, Ahsata Press.

Macmillan Company for "A Commemorative Ode" and "The Seed of Fire" from *Collected Poems, 1924–1974*, copyright © 1974 by John Beecher; "Field and Forest" from *The Lost World*, copyright © 1962, 1965 by Randall Jarrell.

Moore Publishing Company for "That Summer" from *To the Water's Edge* by Sam Ragan; "The Dappled Ponies" from *Coming Out Even* by Campbell Reeves.

Mountain Life and Work for "On Native Ground" by Jim Wayne Miller.

The New Orleans Review for "Continuum," by Kathryn Stripling, copyright © 1974 by Loyola University, New Orleans.

Paul Baker Newman for "Skimmers" from *The Ladder of Love*, The Smith/Horizon Press.

W. W. Norton & Company, Inc., for "Transcendence" from *Diversifications* by A. R. Ammons; "Corsons Inlet" and "Silver" from *Selected Poems* by A. R. Ammons; "Topsoil," "Bees Awater," and "Toolshed" from *Red Owl* by Robert Morgan.

Reynolds Price for "Angel," copyright © 1977 by Reynolds Price.

Random House, Inc., for "Black Children Visit Modern Jail" from *Less than a Score, But a Point* by T. J. Reddy, copyright © 1974, Random House, Inc. (Vintage Books).

Red Clay Books for "New South" and "Wilt" from *East of Moonlight* by Julia Fields; "Morning Stroll" and "Within the Interval" from *Marstower* by Amon Liner; "Moses: A Dialogue" by Adrianne Marcus from *The Moon Is a Marrying Eye*; "The Cremation of R.J." and "Grandmama Jocasta" from *Horse, Horse, Tyger, Tyger* by Heather Ross Miller; "Rap" by Charleen Swansea (Whisnant) from *Eleven*

Charlotte Poets, edited by Robert Waters Grey and Charleen Swansea (Whisnant).

The Sewanee Review (72, 1964) for "Harvey Beaumont's Complaint" by Tom Kirby-Smith, copyright © 1964 by the University of the South.

Simon and Schuster, Inc., for "Nature Study, After Dufy" and "The Oceans of Dr. Johnson" from *When Found, Make a Verse Of* by Helen Bevington.

South Carolina Review for "Primer on Digging" by Dannye Romine.

St. Andrews College Press for "Remembering August 11, The Felix Neck Bird Sanctuary, Martha's Vineyard" from *Mobiles* by Thomas Heffernan; "Scarecrow" and "Newton on Another Day" from *A Sacrifice of Dogs* by William Sprunt.

Tar River Poets for "Anxiety" by Robert Waters Grey from *Sixty North Carolina Poets*.

Thad Stem, Jr., for "Crisis" and "School Days" from *Journey Proud* by Thad Stem Jr., McNally and Loftin.

University of Georgia Press for "Driving through a Country That Is Vanishing," "A Forge of Words," and "Zeppelin Fantasy" from *Statues of the Grass* by James Applewhite; "Sowing Salt" from *Dialogue with a Dead Man* by Jim Wayne Miller.

University of North Carolina Press for "The Man in the Ocelot Suit" and "Wintering" from *Scattered Light* by Christopher Brookhouse; "The Flower-Hunter in the Fields" and "Dealer's Choice and the Dealer Shuffles" from *An Ear in Bartram's Tree* by Jonathan Williams.

University of Pittsburgh Press for "For Malcolm: After Mecca" and "I Called Them Trees" from *Another Kind of Rain* by Gerald Barrax, copyright © 1970.

University Press of Virginia for "A Program for Survival" and "Finding the Pistol" from *A Program for Survival* by Gibbons Ruark.

Wesleyan University Press for "The Night," "To a Fighter Killed in the Ring," and "Cold Water" from *Cold Water*, copyright © 1963, 1964, 1966 by Lou Lipsitz; "It All Comes Together Outside the Restroom in Hogansville" from *Water Tables*, copyright © 1974 by James Seay.

Jonathan Williams for "For George Lewis" from *The Loco Logodaedalist in Situ*, Cape Goliard Press.

The editors also wish to express their gratitude to the North Carolina Arts Council for a grant to aid in preparation of this book.

Contents

Introduction

IN 1932 Allen Tate wrote, "The historian of Southern poetry must constantly pause to enquire into the causes of our thin and not very comprehensive performance. . . ." And his fellow-Fugitive Donald Davidson shared his view: "The arts of the South in times past took another direction than poetry." In this respect North Carolina has been no exception: we have not produced a poet to rank with the novelist Thomas Wolfe, nor has a poet's work had an impact comparable to Paul Green's dramas. The two most famous poets residing in the state have been Carl Sandburg, who wrote little poetry of consequence after moving to Flat Rock, and Randall Jarrell, a latecomer whose poetry is scarcely rooted in the state, or even in the South. A group of poets—most of them non-Southerners—centered around Black Mountain College had a strong influence outside North Carolina but were hardly known inside it. Conversely, our most loved and popular poet, John Charles McNeill, who died in 1907, had only a regional reputation.

But the last two decades have seen an unprecedented explosion of fine poetry in our state. In comparison with most other states, not only is there an unusually large number of people writing poetry here but an unusually large number writing very good poetry. Only two of the poets published in this book, Jarrell and Liner, are dead; many of the others are young and still developing their craft. *Contemporary Poetry of North Carolina* is intended to bear witness to the poetry explosion by providing a representative sampling of what is being written *here* and *now*.

This volume, therefore, with rare exceptions, does not repeat what has been done by previous anthologists. For example, none of the authors in *A Time for Poetry*, edited in 1966 by the North Carolina Poetry Society, have been included. Of the twenty poets in Richard Walser's collection of modern work, *Poets of North Carolina*, published in 1963, fewer than ten appear in this volume. On the other hand, forty-three of the poets we present here are not represented at all in Walser's anthology, and many are being anthologized for the first time. Similarly, we are reprinting only a handful of poems from *North Carolina Poetry: The Seventies*, published in 1975 by the editors as a special issue of *Southern Poetry Review*.

As a matter of fact, it has generally been true of anthologies of Tar Heel poetry that each one collects the work of a new group of poets.

First was *Wood-Notes; or, Carolina Carols: A Collection of North Carolina Poetry*, edited in 1854 by Mary Bayard Larke. The second collection, Hight C. Moore's *Select Poetry of North Carolina*, issued in 1894, brought together poems written since the first anthology. In 1912, E. C. Brooks in *North Carolina Poems* drew almost altogether on contemporary authors. Richard Walser, the state's most diligent promoter of native poets, in preparing editions of *North Carolina Poetry* in 1941 and 1951, was more comprehensive; but when the second edition went out of print and the time for a third came, Walser brought out instead a book of contemporary poetry that was almost entirely new in choice of authors and poems.

The editors of this volume have not wanted to duplicate what has been done before, nor have we wanted to limit the book to a very few poets. Rather, we have tried to include a sample from the work of a considerable number of North Carolina poets (sixty-three to be exact) writing since World War II. And we have used the widest possible latitude in defining "North Carolina poet." The majority of the authors included are—like Thad Stem, John Foster West, and Sam Ragan— native Tar Heels whose work is clearly related to the state. We have also seen fit to include writers who now live out of North Carolina, although they were born and educated here: A. R. Ammons, Gibbons Ruark, Jim Wayne Miller, and Robert Morgan. Similarly we have welcomed as adopted Tar Heels a number who once lived elsewhere but whose writing careers have been located here. Examples are Randall Jarrell, Gerald Barrax, and Lou Lipsitz. With a few obvious exceptions, we have omitted poets who are dead or who are no longer actively writing poetry.

But the wide net we have used in gathering these poems does not completely account for the tremendous improvement we see in recent North Carolina poetry. The main reason will be obvious to anyone who scans the biographies at the back of this book. Most of these poets are professionals, not amateurs; poetry is at the very center of their lives. They are not village versifiers for the county newspaper, specializing in dialect narratives or romantic lyrics and songs such as those anthologized in *The Lyric South* by Addison Hibbard in 1928. These poets have learned their craft not at meetings of a local poetry society but from college courses and hard study and practice; moreover, many of them (most of them, really) teach courses in modern poetry and creative writing. In addition, they influence the tastes of their readers through the editing of magazines and textbooks and by writing articles and reviews. In the 1970s the sentimental sonneteer has been replaced by a sophisticated craftsman. Although verse emerging from academia may exhibit a sameness in theme and technique, it has gained immeasurably in skill and complexity. And there is more originality in these poets' work than there was in the days of verses written on "poetic" subjects in "poetic" diction, not only because the scope of modern poetry is so wide but because each poet writes from a unique sensibility, shaped by the private world he lives in at his deepest level. This new poetry, therefore, displays a startling variety—from the informal and humorous narratives of Fred Chappell to the metaphysical conceptualizing of A. R. Ammons or the pastoral images of Thad Stem.

Such concentration of poetic composition on college and university campuses is anything but peculiar to North Carolina. It is the most obvious aspect of American poetry in general since World War II. (What a change from the days of Carl Sandburg, E. E. Cummings, and Edgar Lee Masters!) What we are seeing is a national trend which is also clearly observable in North Carolina and the South. With rare exceptions poets in this collection are college graduates, most of them holding graduate degrees. In Richard Walser's *Poets of North Carolina* (1963), seven of the twenty poets were teachers; in this book more than two-thirds of the poets represented are English professors (as are the editors).

Perhaps some of the exceptions, those who do not teach English, deserve mention: Sam Ragan, Thad Stem, Harriet Doar, and Dannye Romine are journalists. Julie Suk works for a nature museum. William Sprunt is a practicing radiologist whose poems are colored by his hospital experiences. Furthermore, not all the college professors teach English; Lou Lipsitz teaches political science, J. S. Winkler teaches German, and Harold McCurdy taught psychology. And, of course, some poets have once had occupations other than teaching, sometimes colorful ones: Chuck Sullivan has been a basketball coach and VISTA worker, John Beecher a steel-mill worker and printer, William Harmon a naval officer, and Charles Edward Eaton a diplomat.

Because contemporary North Carolina poets are no longer provincial in their orientation, they adopt the styles and treat the themes that are found throughout the work of present-day poets writing in English. For instance, there is the ironic, self-deprecatory voice, the flatness, and either the discursiveness that is almost prose or the simple statement of the obvious. For discursiveness, note the beginning of Ammons' "Corsons Inlet":

> I went for a walk over the dunes again this morning
> to the sea,
> then turned right along
> the surf . . .

and for straightforward statement see Ann Deagon's "The String Lady":

> This is no yarn I spin: the lady
> is real. Her room is on 46th Street,
> the 9th floor. She has lived there
> for years. This is what she does.

For exact, methodical description in the modern style of showing the object as it is, see Morgan's "Toolshed"—though Morgan is always likely to interject a startling image that gives his poems vibrancy, rather than flatness. Also characteristic of modern poetry is the neo-surrealistic technique that fractures connections in ideas and images; this can be seen throughout these pages but most obviously in Amon Liner's "Within the Interval." Our contemporary fascination with sex, violence, and madness is inevitably reflected in North Carolina poetry: see, for example, Suk's "A Cold Chunk of Star," Lipsitz' "To a Fighter Killed in the Ring," or Liner's "Within the Interval" and Saul's "Diary of a Madwoman."

One notices, too, in North Carolina poetry an awareness of poetic movements all over the world. Since World War II—and this is new— many North Carolina poets have been active in translating poetry, most notably Randall Jarrell, but also Ronald Bayes, Reynolds Price, J. S. Winkler, and others. In this our poets provide a clear contrast to the Charleston poets of the twenties, who were hardly aware of changes taking place in the North and East and were contented to write pale imitations of Sidney Lanier and Edgar Allan Poe. This comparatively new exposure to foreign literature—Oriental as well as European—cannot help influencing our poetry.

But if contemporary North Carolina poets are so much like other modern poets, then why an anthology of North Carolina poetry? Is there anything that can be said to identify poems emanating from this region that don't happen to be about Grandfather Mountain, Cape Hatteras, or the Maco Light? We think there are some generalizations that might be risked, and in the remainder of this introduction we intend to pin down a few characteristics and note some exceptions to them, thereby providing a brief and impressionistic survey of recent North Carolina poetry.

The first statement to be made is that North Carolina poets are seldom observed in the vanguard of today's "experimenters." W. J. Cash in *The Mind of the South* points up the South's conservatism in politics, economics, and religion. As one would expect, the same conservatism is found in Southern poetry, as well as in the other arts. For example, a number of Tar Heel poets adhere to traditional forms and rhythms. Though not so frequently as two decades ago, sonnets and quatrains are still being written in the South. (This would be unthinkable for any member of the current New York School.) Witness here the poems by Hulme, Bevington, Price, and Eaton. Yet to say that North Carolina poetry is conservative is not to say it is in a backwater. Here as in the rest of the country, free verse is now the mainstream of our poetry, particularly in work by younger poets.

It needs to be emphasized that a few poets, such as Jonathan Williams, William Harmon, and Ronald Bayes are obviously experimenting. Williams, a product of the Black Mountain School, has a national reputation as an avant-garde poet. Almost alone among Tar Heel poets he was involved in the Beat movement of the 1950s, and recently he has been producing "found" poems and "visual" poems. A. R. Ammons has experimented with a book-length diary-poem written in short lines on an adding-machine tape. By combining country narratives with formal rhyme schemes, such as *terza rima*, and metaphysical concepts (see "Cleaning the Well"), Fred Chappell is also experimenting. Since no good poet is apt simply to repeat his earlier work, perhaps we should say that North Carolina poets are more *quietly* experimental than American poets generally.

Similarly, the impact of the feminist movement appears less obvious in the work of North Carolina's women poets. "Rap" by Charleen Swansea is the only poem in this anthology that carries a strong sense of a woman's rebellion. In fact, most of the poems by women in this book probably could not be identified as such if the authors' names were blocked out. Poems by North Carolina women which show the influence of feminism tend to express dissatisfaction rather than rebellion and to respond to the feminist movement chiefly by a new freedom to use imagery and subject matter (for instance, menstruation or specific anatomical references) that would have been tabu as recently as ten years ago. In this volume poems by Ann Deagon and Julie Suk assert women's feelings of themselves as sexual beings in a way that is no longer embarrassing.

Another aspect of Southern conservatism is a deep attachment to place, and North Carolina poets exhibit this attachment so often and so emphatically that we must make it a second generalization, rather than a sub-category of the first. Attachment to place has persisted despite the change from an agrarian state to one with industrialized urban centers. The themes inherent in this dramatic change helped bring about the Southern Renaissance of the 1920s and 1930s. The attachment, of course, is to rural and small-town North Carolina rather than Sunbelt suburbia, and it has deepened in this last decade of increasing change and nostalgic fascination with folklore and roots. And as a rule it is an affectionate attachment—in contrast to fiction that exposes the cruelties of farm life, mountain life, or small-town life. In fact, it might be said that we are now seeing a neo-pastoral movement in Southern verse. Thad Stem, for instance, has boasted that he still lives on the same street where he was born, and most of his poems are set in Granville County. Other poets who have tried to capture the scenes and ways of life of their own sections of North Carolina are John Foster West, Jim Wayne Miller, Robert Morgan, and Jonathan Williams in Appalachia; A. R. Ammons and James Applewhite in the tobacco country of the Coastal Plains; and Sam Ragan and Helen Bevington in the Piedmont. Characteristic of North Carolina poems of place are Morgan's "Bees Awater" and West's "Buzzard's Knob." Hunting, fishing, farming are the materials of a number of poems— see Winkler's "Hunt," Chappell's "Farm," Stephenson's "January Hog-Killing," and Jim Miller's "Bee Woman." Finally, Sam Ragan's "That Summer" is a memorable example of a poem planted and rooted in a North Carolina setting.

Allied to the attachment to place is the Southerner's love of storytelling, seen in the work of most of our poets. Fred Chappell's book *River* included a whole series of stories. Narratives or incipient narratives, especially ones about down-home folks, appear throughout North Carolina poetry today, as in the past.

In contrast to the regionalism we have been discussing is the universality of a poet like Randall Jarrell. We do not mean to leave the impression that the typical North Carolina poem would be a narrative of a boy and his dad who fish the creek, prime the tobacco in the north acre, butcher a hog, or hunt a coon. Among the poems included here, Helen Bevington's "The Oceans of Dr. Johnson," Lodwick Hartley's "Struldbrugg," and Sharon Shaw's "For Leonard Woolf" come from their reading, as does Robert Watson's sci-fi poem "Planet Eight." "A Cold Chunk of Star" by Julie Suk and Watson's "Radio Astronomer" are influenced by astronomy, Jonathan Williams' "For George Lewis" by music, Chappell's "Skin Flick" by films, Fields' "Wilt" by sports, and Harmon's "Great Seal" by politics. Obviously, there can be no quintessential North Carolina poem. Subjects such as family and childhood, love and war, are bound to appear—as they do in *all* poetry— and to contrast with individual fantasies and private notions like Applewhite's "Zeppelin Fantasy," Barrax's "I Called Them Trees," and Deagon's "String Lady."

To the variety of subject matter must be added the mixture of tones and techniques—from the wit and polish of Bevington or Hartley, to the free-wheeling satire of Williams or Harmon, to the indignation of Fields and Beecher, to the elusiveness of Adcock and the tentativeness and improvisatory quality of Ammons. It is clear that North Carolina poetry is not limited to "aw-shucks" verse. There is no way to predict what a North Carolina poem will be about or what it will be like. All we can suggest is that there is some likelihood that often it will be about some place in North Carolina.

A poem written by a North Carolinian might also deal with the past, for as William Faulkner said, the past is always with us—and it has not really passed. One of the critical commonplaces about Southern writers is that they often drench their work in a sense of history, frequently relying on local legends and folk motifs. For the Tar Heel poet, the sense of the past informs his work in two ways. First, there is his obvious awareness of the past traditions and modes of his art. As has been suggested, he generally does not repudiate these established traditions, but rather builds on them, adapting old forms and styles to his own needs. Second and more germane here, is the use of the past as material for poetry. Any student of Southern literature notes at once the role of memory in the novels, say, of Thomas Wolfe or Robert Penn Warren, or the plays of Tennessee Williams. It would be surprising if the same were not true of our poets. A number of them seem to return to the time of their childhood as though they did not wish to confront our modern urban and technological society. In any case, Thad Stem and John Foster West often write about the South of the thirties. Sam Ragan's "That Summer" captures the despair of the Depression and his " 'The Prophet' " deals with a vanished way of life. Other poems here have their sources in history, such as Beecher's "Commemorative Ode" and Newman's Bicentennial poem "Washington and the Apes." The Southern poet, we believe, is more likely to turn back to the past than his contemporaries in the East or North.

Had this anthology been compiled a generation ago, religion would have come in for considerable attention. Organized religion is still an important force in North Carolina, but it does not figure significantly in the poems presented here. One reason is that didacticism is no longer fashionable; a more important reason, no doubt, is that most of this generation of poets are humanists. Instead of writing about man's relation to his God, they write about man's relation to man and to his environment. For example, Beecher's "Commemorative Ode," which commemorates the anniversary of a church, is concerned with social rather than theological questions. The church is sometimes used as a source of local color: revival meetings and baptisms. Chuck Sullivan, however, has written a number of poems that reflect his Catholic upbringing. Applewhite's "Forge of Words" treats seriously the strain and tension of a revival meeting. Guy Owen's "My Father's Curse," Reynolds Price's "Angel," and Francis Hulme's "Cherry Tree" are religious poems. But Harold McCurdy's "At Nobska," written in 1958, is the only poem in this book directly concerned with the individual's love for God and celebration of God's creation.

There are, to be sure, many people in North Carolina writing religious verse; there are also a goodly number writing poems expressive of a strong social conscience. Unfortunately, we often admire the message more than the poetic talent involved. For instance, if we have not included much prison poetry, it is not because we are ignorant that it is being written. Actually, we regret that examples of poetry dealing with social concerns are so few in this book. Chuck Sullivan's "Going Rate" and Thomas Walters' "Seton's Folks in Denim Found among Conetoe's First," poems about migrants and sharecroppers, exemplify a sympathy with the poor and a desire to convey to readers the quality of their lives. The only North Carolina poet whose work from beginning to end speaks with energy and indignation for the oppressed of America is John Beecher. Examples of social and political satire, while also rare, are William Harmon's "Great Seal" and Jonathan Williams' "Dealer's Choice and the Dealer Shuffles," both of which are typical of their authors' themes and styles.

Gerald Barrax in "For Malcolm: After Mecca," Julia Fields in "The New South," and Lance Jeffers in "When I Know the Power of My Black Hand" speak for blacks in authentic poems of anger, pride, and anguish. T. J. Reddy's "Black Children Visit Modern Jail" is written directly from his own prison experience. These authors are representative of the black poets now coming to the fore in North Carolina letters—representative, too, in that they do not confine themselves to writing poems about blackness.

Poems about Indian culture also have begun to appear; Marvin Weaver's "Lost Colony" and Kathryn Stripling's "Continuum" are representative examples. No doubt the 1970s will see further development of such themes.

As for the language of these poems, for the most part it is not recognizably North Carolinian; it is not salted throughout with Southern idioms and quaint similes. Yet the varieties of rhythm and language found from Manteo to Murphy do enrich the possibilities of our poetic diction. For example, A. R. Ammons has often used a sophisticated mixture of learned and folksy language. Julia Fields and James Applewhite have written in a poetic black dialect, and John Foster West, Jim Wayne Miller, and Francis Hulme, among others, have made extensive use of their mountain idioms. How such usage can increase the range of language and oppose levels of diction can be seen in Fred Chappell's "Cleaning the Well." "Two worlds there are . . ." the poem begins, and the contrast of worlds is maintained by contrasts of language, constantly played off against one another. "Clean it out good," "Felt I'd fricasseed my ass," "Lord, I sank/Like an anchor" counterpoint passages like

Ice-razors edged
My eyes, the blackness flamed like fever,
Tin became nerve in my hand
Bodiless. *I shall arise never.*

The reader should not be disarmed by the offhand informality of Chappell or the seeming extemporizing of Ammons, for these poets are skillfully drawing on many linguistic resources of which Southern speech is only one. Rarely have contemporary poets composed whole poems in dialect; nevertheless, there is an infusion of Tar Heel language in Tar Heel poetry—certainly enough to warrant mentioning.

To the extent that the ties of a common past, a common territory, and a common speech influence North Carolina poetry, they work also to produce a sense of community among our poets. There is, of course, a sense of community among Southerners generally. The other side of the coin is that there is often a tendency to be exclusive and provincial. There has never been a group in North Carolina comparable to the closely knit Charleston poets or the Vanderbilt Fugitives. However, it is clear that many of these Tar Heel poets have shared experiences with each other and with their readers, that they often know one another and have common interests and ambitions. Some of our poets studied under Randall Jarrell (Heather Ross Miller, Emily Wilson, and Adrianne Marcus, for example). Others are products of William Blackburn's classes at Duke (Chappell, Price, and Applewhite). Another unifying force has been the literary journals published in the state: *Red Clay Reader, Tar River Poets, Greensboro Review,* and *Southern Poetry Review.* Though we have nothing comparable to the fine poetry series issued from Louisiana State University Press and the University of Georgia Press, publishers like John F. Blair, Jonathan Williams' Jargon Press, Charleen Swansea's Red Clay Press, Jackpine Press, The New South Co., The Curveship Press, and Moore Publishing Co. give impressive evidence of the encouragement provided to poetry in this state. Finally, though poets are notorious nonjoiners, many of this state's poets belong to the North Carolina Writers' Conference and other such organizations. The poet, no longer writing in a garret, is no longer a brooding, isolated spirit—if he ever was.

Myths die hard, and we are still confronted with the myth of the poor poet who struggles to find an audience, writing for the most part only for himself and perhaps his friends. In the preface to his 1963 anthology, *Poets of North Carolina,* Richard Walser commented on the difficulty of publication and the lack of remuneration offered to poets. Less than two decades later, the situation is considerably improved, though there continues to be little money in poetry. It is still difficult to find a New York publisher for a volume of poetry by a Southerner, but there are more outlets for poetry than ever before—and here North Carolina clearly leads the South in numbers. One reason for this has been the support provided to literary publications by the North Carolina Arts Council. For example, in 1977 grants were awarded to forty-seven magazines. Poets are also participating in poetry readings across the state, not to mention appearing on radio and TV programs. The Poetry-in-the-Schools Program has helped to support a number of poets, as well as helping to cultivate broader audiences for modern poetry and encouraging poetic composition. In fact, it can be argued that today it is too easy to achieve publication. So much poetry comes from the presses that it is difficult to read it all, or to separate the wheat from the considerable amount of chaff. But this is all part of the current poetry explosion, which it is exciting to be a part of. Certainly if Allen Tate were evaluating North Carolina's "performance" in poetry today, he would pause before labeling it "thin and not very comprehensive."

GUY OWEN AND MARY C. WILLIAMS

*Contemporary Poetry
of North Carolina*

Betty Adcock

WALKING OUT

Fishing alone in a frail boat,
he leaned too far, lost hold,
was turned out of the caulked world.
Seventy years he had lived without knowing
how surfaces keep the swimmer up.

In the green fall, the limbs' churn
of fear slowing to pavane,
one breath held dear as a woman,
he searched for coins of light
in the pockets of terror,
counting oar-strokes backward:
shore was not far.

He did then what was given him to do.
As creatures of water once called on the future
locked in their bodies, he called on his past.
He walked, walked.
Time was enough, just enough, and luck.
Touching greenfingered sand, rising
and touching, the body bursting with useless
knowledge, he came to his height in air.

Back in his life now, he measures
distances one breath long, muses
wordless, flexing the oars of his legs.
    Things shimmer where he is:
    known woods and meadows,
    floors and streets raise walls around him
    the color of old glass.
    Heaven is a high, clear skin.

What he knows paces his green sleep.
All day the world wavers: wife,
sons, friends change.

Age has caught him, they say.
Beneath the drift of flesh his bones remember
trying for bottom.

He walks away.

IDENTITY

> *Men enter by force, drawn like*
> *Jonah*
> *back to their fleshy mothers.*
> *A woman is her mother,*
> *that's the main thing.*
> —ANNE SEXTON

There was a yellow dress with dots,
and once, white shoes with straps.
In a snapshot, black hair merged with shadow,
holding the sick face clear.
I could think I never heard her voice.
                    And that is all
except that I played the Sunday out
with a broken cup and a yellow cat.
                    I remember that
and her name frozen in a stone.
                    I watered it
and flowers planted close as relatives
who stayed. Aunts and cousins bent to kiss
me slowly through years and years,

mouths blooming with pity. They drew me up,
a tight-lipped flower on an only stalk.

Grown now into my life, I own it
like any house freezing the dust love makes
to permanence. My lovers dive and live.
All day I tap messages as though no one could hear,
my voice flaking as stone flakes
in a tangle of underbrush and weather.
In the cold at the clenched heart's center,
the self fails again,
that stranger.

SOUTHBOUND

You can go back in a clap of blue metal
tracked by stewardesses with drinks and virginal masks.
These will work whether you breathe or not. And this
is the first part. The way is farther
into thin roads that sway with the country.
Through the shine of a rented car the red towns rise
and crumble, leaving faces stuck to you like dust.
Following the farms, houses the color of old women,
you gather a cargo from yards full of lapsed
appliances, tin cans, crockery, snapped wheels,
weedy, bottomless chairs. These float through the air
to rest on the sleek hood, the clean seats.
Things broken out of their forms
move to you, their owner, their own.
You slow under weight. The windshield blurs
with the wingbeat of chickens. The hound's
voice takes over your horn.

A green glass vase from a grave in a field,
comes flowerless to your hand, holds a smell
of struck matches, of summer on rust, of running
water, of rabbits, of home.

Then the one place flung up like a barrier,
the place where you stop, the last
courthouse and gathering of garrulous stores.
You have brought the town.
It walks in your skin like a visitor.
Here, under the wooden tongue of the church,
by the paths with their toothed gates,
in the light of the drunk as he burns,
past hunkered children reaching
for the eyes of their fathers, these fading
and coming like seasons,
you are the tall rooms of your dead.

Merchants still ring small furious bells,
and the girl who will does while widows
gossip and curl. Boys still stand
jackknifed to trace deer trails in the dirt,
and black men scythe the lawns, not singing,
keeping their flag hidden.

You may house again these weathers worn thin
as coins that won't spend, worn smooth
as the years between two who are old
and not fooled any longer. You may stand
beneath the Cafe's blue sign where it steps
on the face like a fly. You may bend
to finger the cracked sidewalk,
the shape of stilled lightning, every fork
the same as it was when you meant to follow
that map to the rim of the world.

You may listen for thunder.

A. R. Ammons

SILVER

I thought Silver must have snaked logs
    when young:
she couldn't stand to have the line brush her lower hind leg:
in blinded halter she couldn't tell what had loosened behind her
         and was coming
as downhill
to rush into her crippling her to the ground:

and when she almost went to sleep, me dreaming at the slow plow,
I would
at dream's end turning over the mind to a new chapter
    let the line drop and touch her leg
    and she would
bring the plow out of the ground with speed but wisely
fall soon again into the slow requirements of our dreams:
how we turned at the ends of rows without sense to new furrows
and went back
      flicked by
    cornblades and hearing the circling in
the cornblades of horseflies in pursuit:

      I hitch up early, the raw spot on Silver's shoulder
sore to the collar,
get a wrench and change the plow's bull-tongue for a sweep,
and go out, wrench in my hip pocket for later adjustments,
      down the ditch-path
by the white-bloomed briars, wet crabgrass, cattails,
      and rusting ferns,
riding the plow handles down,
  keeping the sweep's point from the ground,
the smooth bar under the plow gliding,

the traces loose, the raw spot wearing its soreness out
in the gentle movement to the fields:

      when snake-bitten in the spring pasture grass
Silver came up to the gate and stood head-down enchanted
        in her fate
I found her sorrowful eyes by accident and knew:
nevertheless the doctor could not keep her from all
the consequences, rolls in the sand, the blank extension
      of limbs,
      head thrown back in the dust,
useless unfocusing eyes, belly swollen
wide as I was tall
and I went out in the night and saw her in the solitude
      of her wildness:

but she lived and one day half got up
and looking around at the sober world took me back
      into her eyes
and then got up and walked and plowed again;
mornings her swollen snake-bitten leg wept bright as dew
and dried to streaks of salt leaked white from the hair.

CORSONS INLET

I went for a walk over the dunes again this morning
to the sea,
then turned right along
    the surf
        rounded a naked headland
        and returned

   along the inlet shore:

it was muggy sunny, the wind from the sea steady and high,
crisp in the running sand,
    some breakthroughs of sun
  but after a bit

continuous overcast:

the walk liberating, I was released from forms,
from the perpendiculars,
    straight lines, blocks, boxes, binds
of thought
into the hues, shadings, rises, flowing bends and blends
    of sight:

        I allow myself eddies of meaning:
yield to a direction of significance
running
like a stream through the geography of my work:
  you can find
in my sayings
        swerves of action
        like the inlet's cutting edge:

      there are dunes of motion,
organizations of grass, white sandy paths of remembrance
in the overall wandering of mirroring mind:

but Overall is beyond me: is the sum of these events
I cannot draw, the ledger I cannot keep, the accounting
beyond the account:

in nature there are few sharp lines: there are areas of
primrose
    more or less dispersed;
disorderly orders of bayberry; between the rows
of dunes
irregular swamps of reeds,

though not reeds alone, but grass, bayberry, yarrow, all . . .
predominantly reeds:

I have reached no conclusions, have erected no boundaries,
shutting out and shutting in, separating inside
        from outside: I have
        drawn no lines:
        as

manifold events of sand
change the dune's shape that will not be the same shape
tomorrow,

so I am willing to go along, to accept
the becoming
thought, to stake off no beginnings or ends, establish
        no walls:
by transitions the land falls from grassy dunes to creek
to undercreek: but there are no lines, though
    change in that transition is clear
    as any sharpness: but "sharpness" spread out,
allowed to occur over a wider range
than mental lines can keep:

the moon was full last night: today, low tide was low:
black shoals of mussels exposed to the risk
of air
and, earlier, of sun,
waved in and out with the waterline, waterline inexact,
caught always in the event of change:
    a young mottled gull stood free on the shoals
    and ate
to vomiting: another gull, squawking possession, cracked a crab,
picked out the entrails, swallowed the soft-shelled legs, a ruddy
turnstone running in to snatch leftover bits:

risk is full: every living thing in
siege: the demand is life, to keep life: the small
white blacklegged egret, how beautiful, quietly stalks and spears
      the shallows, darts to shore
          to stab—what? I couldn't
   see against the black mudflats—a frightened
   fiddler crab?

     the news to my left over the dunes and
reeds and bayberry clumps was
       fall: thousands of tree swallows
       gathering for flight:
       an order held
       in constant change: a congregation
rich with entropy: nevertheless, separable, noticeable
      as one event,
         not chaos: preparations for
flight from winter,
cheet, cheet, cheet, cheet, wings rifling the green clumps,
beaks
at the bayberries:
    a perception full of wind, flight, curve,
    sound:
    the possibility of rule as the sum of rulelessness:
the "field" of action
with moving, incalculable center;

in the smaller view, order tight with shape:
blue tiny flowers on a leafless weed: carapace of crab:
snail shell:
    pulsations of order
    in the bellies of minnows: orders swallowed,
broken down, transferred through membranes
to strengthen larger orders: but in the large view, no
lines or changeless shapes: the working in and out, together

and against, of millions of events: this,
     so that I make
     no form of
     formlessness:

orders as summaries, as outcomes of actions override
or in some way result, not predictably (seeing me gain
the top of a dune,
the swallows
could take flight—some other fields of bayberry
     could enter fall
     berryless) and there is serenity:

     no arranged terror: no forcing of image, plan,
or thought:
no propaganda, no humbling of reality to precept:

terror pervades but is not arranged, all possibilities
of escape open: no route shut, except in
    the sudden loss of all routes:

     I see narrow orders, limited tightness, but will
not run to the easy victory:
     still around the looser, wider forces work:
     I will try
    to fasten into order enlarging grasps of disorder, widening
scope, but enjoying the freedom that
Scope eludes my grasp, that there is no finality of vision,
that I have perceived nothing completely,
     that tomorrow a new walk is a new walk.

TRANSCENDENCE

Just because the transcendental,
having digested all change into
a staying, promises foreverness,

it's still no place to go, nothing
having survived there into life:
and here, this lost way, these

illusory hollyhocks and garages,
this is no place to settle: but
here is the grief, at least,

constant, that things and loves
go, and here the love that
never comes except as permanence.

James Applewhite

DRIVING THROUGH A COUNTRY
THAT IS VANISHING

It begins to snow in a country
Between the past and what I see,
Soft flakes like eyelids softly descending,
Closing about branches, orchards of pecans,
Like washpot soot streaked in lines on the sky

Or is it that these husks empty of nuts
Are moving upward among the flakes they have suspended,
Like eyesockets gaping or a mockery of birds

So that a girl by the name of Mary Alice Taylor
Sings across this air from the seventh grade.
"Billie he come to see me. Billie he come
Last night." A mole, color of clear skin,
Swims by her nose. Flakes condense the light.

"Billie he asked me to be his wife, 'course I said alright."

Snow as if holding the country houses
Apart to be inspected, unsilvered
Mirror that lets float out of its depths
As from an old ocean of no dimension
Unlimited objects, leather tack and
Spokes of surreys, china
Long broken, whittled horses
Everything their hands would have touched.

A FORGE OF WORDS

I

Moths crowded streetlights revival evenings. The teen-aged
Lingered long outside, reluctantly gathered.
The first hymn calling to sinners, bitter-mellow and lonesome,
Would detach us one by one from circumferences of light:
Circumscribed with shadow by a brim of tin, through leaves
Minnow-live in the wind. Still free among moths, we scraped
The wet sidewalk with reluctant soles, our shoulders flickered
                    over
By magnified wings, like fluttering shapes of our sins.

At last to resist no longer we moved up concrete
Steps, abandoning the afternoon's rain in our thoughts,
To chastise our gesture, flip away bravado like cigarettes.

II

To gather up later. Now to fit sensibly in a pew.
I see my thighs muscled wide in the trousers.
The reverend's eyesockets hollow under eventime lighting.
We weight his voice with our responses; as we bend in singing
We empower his beseeching.
                            Kneeling in shame at the altar,
I sense on the back of my neck that repentance is for women.
I turn and encounter the resolve in masculine faces.
Bill Tyson's leather folds and slab-flat cheeks
From his road-building weather. John Grimsley an ashed-over
            coal,
His face to front the seasons of farming unabashed
By salvation. My own father's jaws locked tight on the names
Of his sins, hardly bowed on his wrestler's neck;
This company of Christians grim like underworld gods.

From the anvil of Christ, I receive my hammered name.

ZEPPELIN FANTASY

I fly on the Hindenburg, though last night
My dreams were of flame. Inside the sound
Of motors in an aluminum piano. Its icy
Tones bare teeth of diamond, whose grin
Chills the bosom of an American heiress.
Languages are eaten with a salad of medals
By the satin stripes of trousers. Girders
Elliptical as sleep invent our night
Above the Atlantic. We dance in a dream
Like a politician's black cigar.

Daphne Athas

ON RETURNING TO NORTH CAROLINA

Two eyes reel across the road
Oysters of the night.
I know I am back home.
They do not recognize me, Odysseus of the Headlights,
Disembodied like my dream.
Black on my paws,
Ears bearing the bearer, listening and slow,
Am I a possum on luminous skates,
A cat? A pig? Behind whose shallow eyes do I lurk?
Or is it they
Who dream I have killed whatever it was
And imbedded the knowledge in velvet by the side of the road?

James Bardon

THE LAST STRAW

With the electric blanket
set at '2,' our mouths
no dryer than peanut brittle

and possibly worse, we
mapped out a night of
awkward encounters first by

rubbing toes, then when
the mood hit
began touching each other

in the dangerous zones.
Warm & willing
you felt like my aunt's

old pillow, a fragrant depository
of skin washed up on
the bed forever, or better yet

the realities of your thigh
keeping me awake all night.
In your room we became

2 match-hungry bottles
of propane gas. We were
jumper cables grappling for

a hot connection.
I can't say anymore about
that room or your brother

dashing in & out
like a track star.
That night we served each other

a generous portion of
ourselves. We
cleaned our plates, cleared

the table & washed our hands
of each other for
good.

Gerald Barrax

FOR MALCOLM: AFTER MECCA

*My whole life has been
a chronology of—changes.*

You lie now in many coffins
in parlors where your name
is dropped more heavily even than Death
sent you crashing to the stage
on which you had exorcised our shame.

In little rooms they gather now
bringing their own memories of your pilgrimage
they come and go
speaking of revolution
without knowing as you learned
how static hate is
without recognizing the man you were
lay in our shame
and your growth into martyrdom.

GHOSTS

Young and talented, they were so good
With words they had lines to throw away
Or they sang and he made any stringed instrument
Do clever things behind, under, or around
Her voice. Their best
Was a thing on death that made it
A kind of fool: they loved each other
So much.

When he started losing her
It was one room at a time
After she'd been the first to learn
She'd watched and felt the rooms changing
Watched her knees unflex
And when her thighs sank below her own horizon
And she saw what he was doing
There the look turned both their bodies to stone and salt.
To be able to let her go
He had to follow her back
Through all the rooms she'd been dying in
And dream she was dead. He dreamed it.
He wrote and sang songs for himself
That would've moved stones or
Death itself if she had been dead.
Then she let him let her go, resurrected
From that house because in everything
They had said whether very clever or merely true
Each would've given back the other's life
To become a stranger in someone else's.
At first he marveled to be still alive until
He walked from room to room in that house
Afraid to ever look back
And learned that death is less than half of dying.

I CALLED THEM TREES

The last time
            I went to the library
I looked at the flowers
surrounding the statue of Stephen Collins

Foster and the old darkie ringing
        the banjo at his feet
                        :flowers planted

in four triangular beds
alternating red and white.
But I saw they were all the same kind.

There were others
                        in front of the building
in long wide rectangular rows
bordered by round clusters of pastel green
and white that were too deep, too dark
            red, maroon, for easy images
                                    :I called
them all flowers.
And the stunted trees I
wished I had known, bending over the green

terrace above the flowers
    like women whose faces
I couldn't see washing
their hair in deep green pools, I called
trees. If I had told you would you
        have known them?
                            There were
flowers for me. There
were trees. There were kinds
of birds and something blue

that crouched
                in the green day waiting
for evening.
If I had told you would
you have known?

So I sat
        on a bench among flowers
and trees facing
the traffic   surveying all

I knew of impalas, cougars, falcons
        barracudas, mustangs, wild
                                cats
marlins, watching cars
go by.   I named them
        all.

Susan Bartels

CONTRASTS

What kind of death
crawls from under these familiar rocks
lichen covered in perpetual shade?
Here copperheads wind among the creek banks
following half caves where clay
is cut under, forming precarious ledges
along the shore.
Spiders, marked and ominous,
inhabit rock gardens near the house.
We step carefully in night grass
never barefoot.

There we hear of rattlers
but have never seen them.
We lie in long grass
where the wind makes waves
halfway between two oceans,
watch insects crawl on green stalks.

The black earth, moist in our hands,
beneath our feet,
is furrowed to cradles.
Digging is easy.
What the land absorbs
it holds
by deep filaments.

Ronald H. Bayes

THE PHILADELPHIA AIRPORT

Rather tired at the Philadelphia airport.
And the plane to board
an hour and three coffees away.

What irony that at five-thirty A.M.
I am at last moved by emotion
(it has been a long time) when
the unavoidable, continual soft-music loudspeaker
romps a certain German polka,

And I remember another airport,
other years,
and I who have never wished to go back before
wish to go back.
But one never can in time
(and does space matter much?).
Want some irony?
In Germany it was—you weren't there—
and I loved you: Christ! with what passion
of intensity; jealous of whomever you were with

With the dawn pink and blue and grey and
the trees mushroom clumping
like wanting Breughel
to red-in country rompers—or
maybe someone good at satyrs—
And I remember that other airport,
I remember a polka
and that I loved you.

Now each in maze muddled and adjusting
and we no longer love. Why kid? And I am not
even jealous in wild imaginings.

A few people,
a few more people:
now we move . . . you move . . . I move . . . from progress
to progress,
unlove to unlove,
anticipating only departures.

John Beecher

A COMMEMORATIVE ODE

*For the 60th Anniversary of the Beecher Memorial
United Church of Christ in New Orleans, Louisiana,
October 25, 1964*

Old church with the same name as my own
you and I were born in the same year
It has taken two generations to bring us together
Now here we are in New Orleans
meeting for the first time
I hope I can say the right thing
what the man you are named for
might have said on one of his better days
He was my great-great-uncle
but come to think of it
he was instrumental in my founding too
Rolled in a tube at home I have a certificate
signed by Henry Ward Beecher
after he had united my grandfather and grandmother
in the holy bonds of matrimony
at Plymouth Church in Brooklyn
The year was 1858
and James Buchanan was President
The South was riding high
making the North catch and send back its escaped Negroes
and it looked to most people
as if slavery were going to last forever
but not to Henry Ward Beecher
which I suppose is why you named your church for him
He certainly helped to change all that
together with his brother Edward and his sister
whose name was Harriet
and Mr. Lincoln and General Ulysses S. Grant
and a large number of young men

who wound up under the long rows of crosses
at Gettysburg Chickamauga Cold Harbor and such places

Nineteen hundred and four was a better year
than 1858
and the building of this church was a sign of it
It was no longer a crime to meet and worship by yourselves
with your own preacher
your own beautiful songs
with no grim-lipped regulators to stand guard over you
nobody breaking up your services with a bullwhip
Yes this was some better
Booker T. Washington was in his heyday
the apostle of segregation
"We can be in all things social as separate as the fingers"
he said and Mr. Henry Grady the Atlanta editor
applauded him to the echo
as did all the other good white folks around
and they said
"This boy Booker has a head on his shoulders
even if it is a nappy one"
Dr. Washington was 48 years old at the time
but you know how southern whites talk
a man is a boy all his life if he's black
Dr. Washington was a pragmatist
and settled for what he could get
When they announced that dinner was served in the dining car
he ate his cindery biscuits out of a paper bag
and when George the porter made up berths in the Pullman
he sat up all night in the Jim Crow coach
Because of his eminently practical attitude
Dr. Washington was successful in shaking down
the big white philanthropists
like C. P. Huntington the railroad shark
or was it octopus
and Negro education was on its way

Old church
since 1904
you and I have seen some changes
slow at first
now picking up speed
I have just come from Mississippi
where I saw churches like this one
burned to the ground
or smashed flat with bombs
almost like Germany when I was there in 1945
only these Negroes were not beaten people
They sang in the ashes and wreckage
such songs as *We Shall Overcome*
and *Let My Little Light Shine*
O Freedom! they sang
Before I'll be a slave
I'll be buried in my grave
and go home to my Lord and be free
They sang *I'm going to sit at the welcome table*
I'm going to live in the Governor's mansion
one of these days
I heard three mothers speak
who had made the President listen
and "almost cry, or he made like he was about to cry"
when they told him
how their homes had been dynamited
"It's not hard to be brave"
one of these mothers said
"but it's awful hard to be scared"
I expect to see her statue on a column in the square
in place of the Confederate soldier's
one of these days

Remember
slavery looked pretty permanent in 1858
when it had just five years to go

and now in 1964
the White Citizens' Councils and the Ku Klux Klan
think they can keep their kind of half-slave South forever
Their South isn't on the way out
It's already dead and gone
only they don't know it
They buried it themselves
in that earthwork dam near Philadelphia Mississippi
when they thought they were getting rid of the bodies

THE SEED OF FIRE

For Highlander Folk School

The celluloid is old. It snaps and must
be spliced. The worn-out sound track garbles words.
But here they are, the marching union men,
the girls with banners. Pitiful! A torrent
of mountain water plunging from the rocks
to lose itself downstream in stagnant sloughs,
mud-clogged meanderings and stinking pools.
The nation rots. What we were once looks out
of this old film with shining eyes. Where did
we miss our way? New men rise up with skins
dark-hued to take the vanguard place of those
grown compromised and well content to rake
fat winnings from the gamble of death. Dark too
those women who indomitably face
plantation lords and teach sea-island folk,
disfranchised all their voiceless lives, to stand
and vote. Here is the continuity,
the precious seed of fire in these sad ashes.

Helen Bevington

VISIT TO NEFERTITI

The only lady I've ever seen
With two cracked ears and one eye missing
Is Akhenaten's luminous Queen

Nefertiti. What girl would risk it,
Wearing upon her head a crown
In shape like a wastepaper basket?

Whose other eye is pure rock crystal,
Painted a shade of brown like Swiss
Chocolate or a female kestrel?

And yet the lady glitters gold,
Flawless as apricots in sunshine,
So young, at thirty centuries old,

Her name "The Beautiful One Is Come"
Is how she struck me—blindingly
Herself in the Staatlichen Museum.

NATURE STUDY, AFTER DUFY

When a friend accused Dufy of playing
fast and loose with nature,
he replied: "But nature, my dear Sir,
is only an hypothesis."

I must remember to dismiss
These wintry skies that seem to me
Not gray, like an hypothesis,
But silver, like reality—
This arguable wind that stirs
So plausibly the conifers.

From postulates of days, unwary,
By seeming snows preoccupied,
I have conjectured January
And whiteness in the countryside,
Presumed the starlings in the holly.
I must remember now as folly

What earlier instants of surmise?
(The earth, one green and passing minute,
The poplar gold before my eyes,
The summer beech with sunlight in it—
These that by leaflessness of bough,
By empty fields, are proven now

Untenable, as soon must be,
With the first inference of spring,
This crystal world, this theory.)
I must be quick in questioning
The look of April after this
When it too is hypothesis.

THE OCEANS OF DR. JOHNSON

I never take a cup of tea
But I consider pleasurably
That, poured a twenty-seventh cup,
Dr. Johnson drank it up.

Before that mighty thirst was quenched,
Pot by pot, his hostess blenched
And, marveling, took fearful count
To be exact in the amount.

Perhaps his dryness had diminished,
Say, when the twenty-first was finished,
Yet being in a social mood
He drank to thrust out solitude,

Extending the complacent hour,
The festive rite, by staying power.
And twenty-seven cups would be
His limit, his capacity.

Christopher Brookhouse

THE MAN IN THE OCELOT SUIT

Our neighbor's dog ate
Our paper. My wife
Complained. They said get up
Earlier, go to work.

What do you do all night?
My wife said
We think grave thoughts, and laugh
Against establishments.

The dog kept eating the paper,
So I rented
An ocelot suit and sprang
Out of a ditch. The terrified

Dog never came back,
But our neighbors
Came, breathing hard, and ate
The paper themselves to set

Us straight and make the world
Safe from crackpots.
Now I loaf in my sleek
Ocelot suit, amusing the children.

When it is night,
I leap onto our neighbor's
Roof and devour their dreams.

WINTERING

There are eyes among the sedge,
And eyes along the branches,
And eyes that peer above
The slate flatness of the pond,
And all these eyes watch
The drift of scattered light.

A few late birds beat south.
They are lost in the sky like smoke
Blown from my stone chimney.
The hills are vast and silent.
Snow will fall soon; the deer
Will nudge my door to lick

Salt from my hand; and beasts
Will turn from their solitary hunts
And sleep in the warm shadows
Of their enemies. And I
Will sit at the edge of fire.
I will be safe from cold.

But my knife shines in my hand:
How easy to slice this flesh
And watch it open and spread.
I will hear the long breathing
From the deep dens of animals.
I winter in my own shadow.

Fred Chappell

'THE FARM

The hay, the men, are roaring on the hill, July
Muzzy and itchy in the field, broad sunlight
Holds in its throat the tractor's drone, dark bees
Like thumbs in the white cut bolls of clover.
Summer in the fields, unsparing fountain
Of heat and raw savor. Men redden and boil
With sweat, torsos flash, talk, and the laughing
Jet up cool, single cool sound in saffron air,
Air like a yellow cloak. The land is open,
At the mercy of the sky, the trembling sun and sky.
One cloud drives east. Cattle plunder the brackish pools,
Drop awkward shadows while black flies fumble on their skins;
Ruminate; and observe the hour with incurious eye.

The mouths of the men are open, dark medals dangling.
They gulp fierce breath. If a breeze lift the field, skins cloy
With dust. Grin and gouge; neck muscles first tire;
Exhaustion laps the bodies, the mouths are desperately open.
The woman brings water, clear jar echoing
Rings of light fluttering on her apron. Wagon heaped,
    bronze-green
Shaggy hay like a skirt about it, halts then sways
Gingerly to the barn. Bronze-green tongues of it leap
To the sill; harry it in and the loft is bulging, loft
Surfeited beneath the tin roof of fire. Mouse-gray
Pigeons march, dipping beaks like shards of flower pots.

. . . And the hill bared for the blackbirds, swoop in a
    burst net,
Scattered like pepper specks; men, shouts of flesh, gone
Home, to the wash basins, to tables glowing
With victual. Slow dark enfolds them all, mountains

Empurple and encroach.
                                    Hay away, tobacco then and
Corn as the ground dies and cools and barns huddle
In weird light, bats in the gray dusk like pendulums.
Goldenrod indolent, blue moonlets of chickory, Queen
Anne's lace precise as the first stars of frost. Ponds
Grimace and show their teeth under a wind slicing southeast.

The land is puckered and now not open.

Trees thrash, noble and naked wrestlers. Clouds
Mass in the high winds. Birds go away, the shining
Ones, but quail and bobwhite keep the earth. Grass
Graying, thistleweed spending its baubles, frost drives
Deep into rind and pith. The brittle season. Crash crash
Of leaves in seemly groves; late-sweet austerity; blue grapes;

Last glimmer of crickets.

Then winter in the hearth, snaps and snaps
Like cap-pistols the sizzling oak joint and the smoke
Goes bare under the sky. The grandfather snorts
And nods and the chessboard idles while whiskey
Nudges his elbow. All rooms grow smaller, the house
Tightens and the roof howls. Creak creak
The timbers mutter. Ice like cheesecloth on still waters.
Glass needles in the ground. Clear rime. Rattles; clinks;

Stupor of cold wide stars.

And winter in the constricted fields, wind from dead
North mauling the cattle together, furrows hides
Red and white, sifts into the creases fine snow
Like moss; they moan at the gates, turning the helpless eye.
Barns let the blow in, spaces between boards
Crusted slick, sleet piddles the foil-like roofs.
The sky a single gray smear and beneath it flesh

Pinches and rasps, reluctant in unyielding skin . . .
Sun, blind on the first deep snow, every edge
Departs nature, revealing its truthful contour;
Nothing is stark now. The light enlarges and enlarges
Such a fearful blue the head is pained, and burns;
And the body feels evanescent as mist. Sky cloudless,
Birdless, merciless.
                         Night closes over, deep
Crucible; land creeps to star-marge; horizon
Cluttered with light, indifferent emblem of eternity.

Nothing will move but the sauntering wheel of sky

Axis that fixes and orders rolling slowly on a hub of ice.

The houses burrow deeper and deeper.

The world, locked bone.

SKIN FLICK

The selfsame surface that billowed once with
The shapes of Trigger and Gene. New faces now
Are in the saddle. Tits and buttocks
Slide rattling down the beam as down
A coal chute; in the splotched light
The burning bush strikes dumb.
Different sort of cattle drive:
No water for miles and miles.

In the aisles, new bugs and rats
Though it's the same Old Paint.

Audience of lepers, hopeless and homeless,
Or like the buffalo, at home
In the wind only. No
Mushy love stuff for them.

They eye the violent innocence they always knew.
Is that the rancher's palomino daughter?
Is this her eastern finishing school?

Same old predicament:
No water for miles and miles,
The horizon breeds no cavalry.

Men, draw your wagons in a circle. Be ready.

CLEANING THE WELL

Two worlds there are. One you think
You know; the Other is the Well.
In hard December down I went.
"Now clean it out good." Lord, I sank
Like an anchor. My grand-dad leant
Above. His face blazed bright as steel.

Two worlds, I tell you. Swallowed by stones
Adrip with sweat, I spun on the ache
Of the rope; the pulley shrieked like bones
Scraped merciless on violins.
Plunging an eye. Plunging a lake
Of corkscrew vertigo and silence.

I halfway knew the rope would break.

Two suns I entered. At exact noon
The white sun narrowly hung above;
Below, like an acid floating moon,
The sun of water shone.
And what beneath that? A monster trove

Of blinding treasure I imagined:
Ribcage of drowned warlock gleaming,
Rust-chewed chain mail, or a plangent
Sunken bell tolling to the heart
Of earth. (They'd surely chosen an art-
less child to sound this soundless dreaming

O.) Dropping like a meteor,
I cried aloud—"Whoo! It's *God
Damn* cold!"—dancing the skin of the star.
"You watch your mouth, young man," he said.
I jerked and cursed in a silver fire
Of cold. My left leg thrummed like a wire.

Then, numb. Well water rose to my waist
And I became a figure of glass,
A naked explorer of outer space.
Felt I'd fricasseed my ass.
Felt I could stalk through earth and stone,
Nerveless creature without a bone.

Water-sun shattered, jelly-
bright wavelets lapped the walls.
Whatever was here to find, I stood
In the lonesome icy belly
Of the darkest vowel, lacking breath and balls,
Brain gummed mud.

"Say, Fred, how's it going down there?"
His words like gunshots roared; re-roared.
I answered, "Well—" (*Well well well . . .*)
And gave it up. It goes like Hell,
I thought. Precise accord
Of pain, disgust, and fear.

"Clean it out good." He drifted pan
And dipper down. I knelt and dredged
The well floor. Ice-razors edged
My eyes, the blackness flamed like fever,
Tin became nerve in my hand
Bodiless. *I shall arise never.*

What did I find under this black sun?
Twelve plastic pearls, monopoly
Money, a greenish rotten cat,
Rubber knife, toy gun,
Clock guts, wish book, door key,
An indescribable female hat.

Was it worth the trip, was it true Descent?
Plumbing my childhood, to fall
Through the hole in the world and become . . .
What? *He told me to go. I went.*
(Recalling something beyond recall.
Cold cock on the nether roof of Home.)

Slouch sun swayed like a drunk
As up he hauled me, up, up,
Most willing fish that was ever caught.
I quivered galvanic in the taut
Loop, wobbled on the solid lip
Of earth, scarcely believing my luck.

His ordinary world too rich
For me, too sudden. Frozen blue,
Dead to armpit, I could not keep
My feet. I shut my eyes to fetch
Back holy dark. Now I knew
All my life uneasy sleep.

Jonah, Joseph, Lazarus,
Were you delivered so? Ript untimely
From black wellspring of death, unseemly
Haste of flesh dragged forth?
Artemis of waters, succor us,
Oversurfeit with our earth.

My vision of light trembled like steam.
I could not think. My senses drowned
In Arctic Ocean, the Pleiades
Streaked in my head like silver fleas.
I could not say what I had found.
I cannot say my dream.

When life began re-tickling my skin
My bones shuddered me. Sun now stood
At one o'clock. Yellow. Thin.
I had not found death good.
"Down there I kept thinking I was dead."

"Aw, you're all right," he said.

Ann Deagon

MOVING NORTH

The Brown Recluse, also known as the Hermit Fiddler, a spider whose bite produces a gangrenous sore, is apparently spreading northward. From its original home in the Southwest it has now migrated as far as North Carolina.

Not it. She. The one with eggs.
Demographer with the future in her belly,
moving up in the world. Texas rots
dry, Louisiana wet. Twenty
years in Alabama: closets, drawers,
silver chests, the backs of portraits
cottoned with eggs and everywhere the sweet
festering scent. In Tennessee
she homed into the woodpile, roughed it,
budded the boards with eggs. Now here
holed up in my ornamental block
she babysits a quiet contagion.

                        Lady,
I know your bite. I am myself
something of a recluse and given
to wearing brown. My Odyssey—
no, my Penelopeid up the dry
shins of girlhood to the wetter parts
was not unlike your own. We are heading
both of us north. The cold, I hear,
is shriveling, the cold bites back.
Even in this lush midway state I feel
a touch of gangrene on my hither leg,
some deadlier hermit fiddling in my brain.

THE STRING LADY

The string lady is in her room.
She has unraveled the city.
Great hanks snarls ravelings
of twine net her. She is a salty
catch, an octopus untangling
America. She rolls it up. Balls
orbit her like moons. They snowball.

This is no yarn I spin: the lady
is real. Her room is on 46th Street,
the 9th floor. She has lived there
for years. This is what she does.
Why did she begin? Did she
watch a beachcomber shoulder
a great rope, its frayed end
down his back like a mane
raveled to ringlets? Or
on Sunday morning opening
the broom closet found the roomer
with an extension cord close
around his throat? She does not say.

It gets harder to find string.
Soon the world will come unstrung.
Then she will unravel the drapes
the bedspread her socks sweater
underwear her white hair her skin
coarse threads slubbed with moles
then her stringy flesh veins tendons
wound round. Last the ganglia
the spinal cord—oh Ariadne's clue
out of the labyrinth and all it takes
is winding! She winds down

the last spidery ball. The room
is in order. The room waits.

After a thousand years or so, listen:
Do the balls stir? Is something
beating   like a heart?

TOD UND DAS WEIB

No flowers. I will not lie
in state or under the astroturf
of cemeteries. (Earth has been
often enough my bed, but with
livelier bedfellows than these
morticians.) I have other plans.

I am engaged to Johns Hopkins.
Packed in that cool drawer
I hold my breath. My new lovers
scrub up. They clip their nails.
They put rubbers on their fingers.
They make jokes. They will uncover
all my secrets. They will know me
inside out.

I do not say all love is like this.
But if it is I choose it still:
as I came naked from my mother
as I went naked to my man
to feel at dying as at borning
against my flesh in their sweet fumble
the brash tentative hands of men.

Harriet Doar

THE POOL

each in his element   but
                    what is mine?
the snakebird coolly gliding under water
and squirrels
                    fluid quicksilver from branches
flicker   like jays   the blue flash
                    in the sun
weaves through the leaves   and clouds above them move
wind-drifting   towering   luminous   their sails
gathering light that glances off the trees'
leaf-tremble
                    in the water   fishes arc
ripple   mobile   turned by braided currents
sun-shadowed   gray-green-brown   the hazel-eyed
in which I see a faint translucent image
the upside-down   the drowned   the inward   sky
in which birds fly   leaves flicker   under water
troubled my self   what is your element?

THE GIFT

Now he has a cat's-eye to explore
The dark, the moth night beyond his door.
The shadow wings brush close, but he disdains
To shrink the shadows back into their skins
Or bend the shaft to probe for knuckled roots
That lurk to clutch the unenlightened foot
And pitch him on his face and claw his knees.
He is impatient with his yesterdays

That kept him rayed within the cabin's arc;
His frail light pulls him onward through the dark.
He moves alone beyond protected years
To lean an arrogant question on the stars.

Charles Edward Eaton

THE GOOSE

It will not do, it will not do, to say you are a giver
Of life, a life-enhancer, if you expect undue return
Like the man force-feeding the goose to fatten up his liver.

Clutched like a wine skin with a curious beaked spout,
The goose submits, rapt with ecstasy, abuse, his wide eye
    staring like a drop of wine,
Insane to know how food in such an orgy came about.

The man is very powerful, very efficient with his funneled
    grinder.
One must reach well down into the gullet to avoid choking
    or regurgitation—
If the eye is bloodshot, well, that may serve the goose as
    blinder.

It does not matter, if you are that force-feeder, what you say:
The goose is mindless, does not know if you are good or bad—
You give him his loathsome debauch to yield the best paté.

Which one of us has not been throttled for his good,
The common good, and waddled, bruised, stupefied, away,
Feeling giddy yet beheaded, all bottom like a glutted sack,
    burdened and misunderstood?

I am told the goose will find a way out in disease,
Posing a morbid but authentic answer on a cracker—
It will not do, it will not do, to say you aim to please.

GIRL RAKING HAY

In what she will look like ten years from now
I am not interested, and cannot afford to be.
She may be latent with guilt, sorrow, vice,
Lurking like an X-ray time will develop.
I want her as she is, pure and simple,
In her white dress and broad-brimmed, straw sunhat
Raking hay slowly on a summer day.
The body may have its hidden bullet
Already—that too the X-ray will disclose:
Someone she loves, hates, someone she envies—
Erotic, without consequence, I want her
As a poured out picture that slowly moves,
Back, forth, no further than a windshield wiper,
Both proud and limited, and just for me—
She will never know how I have used her,
Heaping up my nerves in dense, tawny mounds
Her rake moves through like a thick, dulcet comb,
How I am so charged with the bright, brutal—
Mold from the dungeon, musk of sexual thrust,
A much too rapidly developing picture,
A roomful of poses, an expelled history—
One stark, tremendous contention remains,
The lucid picture that hides in the sun.
One sees it even on dark, rainy days,
Clearing, back and forth, so far, no further—
You may call it illicit, this looking,
This lying down to the rake's long fingers.
But I can only tell you that I feel
Exposed, exposed, without ruin or record,
Imprinted with something I call myself.

THE IMAGE ON THE KNEE

Ask for that late, last sensuous friend, and you may find him,
    undeploring, undeplored,
Lifting the view of a luminous sea as if it were a golden cup,
Or standing, drinking wine, eating fruit at some exquisite sideboard.

Which is to say in knowing how to make the large look small,
The small loom large, he is an ardent man in any house:
Ask for that one who's been around the tracks so much—You find
    a tremulous racer in a stall.

He moves somewhere between the lavish sea, the lucent fruit—
Let him prowl, pry into your much picked over life a while,
And even there he finds the nacreous or the nectared drop,
    a thimbleful of loot.

Since almost any friendship, as it wears, debases,
We wonder what the secret of this loafer, lounger, is,
And with the worst will in the world would shout in that pink
    ear: Get down to cases!

Just at that point, he shuts up shop, collapses sideboard, sea,
Much as a Sunday painter closes for the week his leaching box
    of paints,
Or some ventriloquist removes an image strangely like our simulacrum
    from his knee.

He has gone somewhere else—A cosier view, a better light—
In these days when our deliverers are late, last, and, oh, so few,
Someone had better go out looking for him—You go left, I go right.

Julia Fields

NEW SOUTH

Tired
> old phoenix
> > chokes on
> > > ashes,
> > > walks through . . .
> > > > crimson.

Lynching trees
> > charred
> > bend
> > toward . . .
> > > progress

Violence sleeps in fret
> strait laced in rhetoric.
> midnight smells of blood:
> Day light is cool bloodtide . . .
> > crimson.

The wolves are laughing in the woods—
for the new phoenix
> > who is choked with ashes
> > the wolves are waiting near the woods.

˙WILT

is
the
forest negro
lion man
giraffe

heads above all heads,
hands above all hands

leaping

arcs and amps of fire
churning power to

grace.

locomotive man.
engine man.
capsule man.
set down upon this chained land.

rippling

old king with the
rust-colored toy.
what will the new
time do with you?
king Tut on the
faultline of freedom.

when you walk, it is
the fluid stalk of
all origination.
old king with the
rust-colored balloon-
prop for airy stagecraft.
what will the new
time do to you?

Robert Waters Grey

ANXIETY

When it cuts invisible paths through flesh and bone
to squeeze and rub bare strips of nerve
the house goes stiff—
unable to fly   the wings
at strict right angles
mimic flight.
Inflexible   it will not creak.
Old footsteps on worn stairs
do not warp wood.
Wind backs from window cracks.
Numb insects die to stings.
Glass dims.
Tin burns to rust.
Brick rots.

As it drifts from room to room
flowers turn from the sun.
Chairs become arthritic.
Silence sucks the sap from weathered strips.
Dust hides under dust.
Beagles claw torn screens.
A grandfather clock
strikes monotones.

Words thicken and fall in the dark.
Failing eyes spin darkness from the light.
Lungs freeze.
The heart denies its pump.

O. B. Hardison, Jr.

IF YOU GOTS TO ASK
YOU NEVER GETS TO KNOW

What is it, Why?
People ask questions like that before, not after.
After, they have whatever answers there are.

Here is one:
You cannot leave this room without leaving it.
When you have gone you cannot come back.
You will see it in terms of next door.
There will be a different dandelion on the wallpaper.
When you look back, this room, which has all the shades half drawn,
Will be shaggy and golden.

If not, you would have no way of knowing.
Nobody gets anywhere without going.
If you are on a high wire: somersault.
If running from a freight train: dance.
If holding your own: wrestle it to the ground.

Next door is good because you will be in it.
In a sense, you are there already.
Even now, its dandelions sway to your shadows.
Soon everything will be obvious.
There will not be a single metaphor in all your sentences.
Whatever you say will be understood.
Already you know how it feels to be shaggy and golden,
And what it is to walk on a high wire and to run from a freight train
        and to hold on to what you are.
Risk everything now.
Next door you will meet one, two, three.

ROOM WITH ELEMENTS

Here in this room filled with leaving,
Sunlight on the bare floor,
A space almost empty,
You, most perfectly, are.
Earth, air, fire, and water be your elements,
And I your element.

I think how the bright sea extends its arms to the land
(The loving sea)
And falls back, and returns,
And falls back, and again, so you to me.

I, mariner, my boat obscure, explore
(But for one star lost, but that star fixed most truly at the center)
Most amazed, unmeasured you, through all those elements.

Earth: the dust that trembles at your touch.
Air: the dazzled air through which you move.
Fire: that turns the blood to smoking gold
(Most gentle fire). Water: it is your name.

Reach and touch me.
Leave, and return, and return, again and again.
Surround me, and in surrounding, as air in fire,
Be wholly light.

So shine that no darkness is.
All gold, and perfect be; be only splendor.
Never waver, for all know (for it must happen)
That all lights, even those most cherished,
Made of those mortal elements—
And for this most cherished are—are owed to darkness.

William Harmon

THE DAWN HORSE

Again the time and blood consuming sun crosses its corner
with a web of new born light
and there the last stars literally starve

Grey among a hundred or so other greys
the dawn horse stirs

wakes to the waking manifold of new circumstance
and—totally inhuman and remote
among deep empty drums of sound unreeling hungrily
    as though long drowned or long ago
      among unsteady equinoctial darknesses—
stands

On the welcoming west slope of the world's first mountain
half dark in the tilted dominion of imperial light and common grasses
he is standing up
    as dew will stand on the pitched deck of grass
    difficult in the looking light

an ordinary model of simplicity
spotted
    as when water spots a smooth leaf
    with many magnifying glasses
    that evaporate in place
    or else slip in the inflammatory turn and sloping
cold
solid enough for anybody

Not one that waits at a fence for forked hay
or feedbag of fodder hung on a headstall in a stable

it is only he
the ghostly dawn horse
not maiden white but stone colored

Not a martingale gnawing nightmare
or rainbow shouldered unicorn at ironic attention
but a shaking shadow
    like the remote beating of the timed beast heart
begotten and blessed by something
blooded and blood loving

    Lowering his head for a moment
he starts to step

MOTHSONG

Some dust,

such as it is,
is transferred from a mother's album
to a son's turning finger,

then from the finger
to the front of a dark coat,
once a father's,

and then from there, some months later,
to the substance that is found
on a newborn moth's wing,

witnessed intermittently from below
colliding fitfully with the frosted globe
of a fixture
in the middle of a kitchen ceiling,

an irregular but redundant disturbance,
turning, stubborn,
a tolling of sorts, or
a knocking,

like something asymmetrical happening,

the song of an old fork
going downstairs.

And so from that moth now
back to this paper,
not so far after all
from the heavy black pages
of a mother's album under a table lamp,

bland public paper
here in the hand,
to be balled up,

a fist, a mind,
a clenched white apple
hanging in a darkening orchard.

THE GREAT SEAL

There is (dear Mother) this Thing socketed in our general ear,
an acoustic plug piped into the corner pocket of the switchboard-spigot
    of American history's ballistic hydrant,
the shimmering whisper of 200 candles parading in step on the frosted
    ground of a modest cake,
firedrops that share the daily air & consume by illuminating the book
    of comic hours, *novus ordo seclorum.*

Sing, Smith-&-Wesson, Siamese muse of political science,
the freeze-dried skeleton of Coolidge, a box of jewel-mounted bones
    sleeping soundly, soundlessly,
camel-chinned Hawkeye with a jigsaw jaw
budging page by ledger page
down the banjo-tight arteries of the Atlantic seaboard,
his administration a nacelle of silence,
a jumbo dim republican balloon
for interstellar Calvin, now a god, like Caesar, Cesare, Kaiser, Tsar,
    Marshal, Chairman, Paraclete;

& of wide-shouldered Eisenhower
smiling amid the paradise of Dwights,
putting, bidding seven spades, painting,
each landscape Normandy, each flawless day a recapitulated 6th of June;

& the American Legion on celestial parade behind the elite of the Forty
    & Eight in their synthetic locomotives,
Arlington's bumper crop all perfectly in step,
gold & purple garrison caps catching the tracer light,
Shriners goosing teenage majorettes with cattle-prods (it's all for
    charity),
fake Moslems at both poles, Mason versus Panther,
both plagued houses imprisoned in the many mansions of their universe
    of symbols
ignited at night, seats scorching down a lubricated banister of words,
words abundant & meaningless
as hydrogen bijoux explode
above and screaming jay-colored Atlantic & Pacific schools.

Lodwick Hartley

STRULDBRUGG

One scarcely knows
how to do these days:
remembering is not easy,
forgetting is,
and youth goes by barefoot
with dirty stringy hair,
sometimes bearded in the male
to make the difference easier.
And the streets are long and hard,
the joints are tender,
full of pain,
the air full of stuff
that clogs the nostrils,
chokes the throat.
And the television's blue light
of life-true color
dithers on in the long evenings,
accompanying the idiot chant
given out sidewise
to bleary eyes and a dull brain.

Thomas Heffernan

REMEMBERING AUGUST 11,
THE FELIX NECK BIRD SANCTUARY,
MARTHA'S VINEYARD

I could begin by saying, Felix Neck
Was the last place we went, a foraging goose
Following us like a pointing bird dog, the peacock
Shimmering among pines beyond the other geese.
I could begin by saying, The wild turkey cock
And his hens ate our cereal just after dawn;
Leaving we heard the grasses sigh; they spoke
Time leaning grey to us then green again.
A brook I bestrode curved between arched banks,
I could begin, saying the furled oak, like a tree
Grown in China, leaned from the landward bank
Toward the silvery water from the sea
Between the Neck and the Beach Causeway: all play
Back, will begin again, that dawn, that day.

Gill Holland

NO FORWARDING ADDRESS

(to J. S. W., poet-fisherman)

I knew Izaak Walton in the sixties
and rising seventies
when he was casting every sentence
far out to the inevitable moment
the line turned to muse's tangled maenad hair

he pulled it in wet
with a colored fly left high over the stream
to be cut free like words from a dictionary
from flannel canvas and the felt hat of a fellowfisherman

flies bright in the palm
fast in the stream
each cast was always meant for the big one
though in our day the sixties and rising seventies
his soul knows what passes now for fishing
is fishy
art arty

the white water's finished
there's only friendly fellows
that like their fish like their words
tame and on a platter

Francis Pledger Hulme

CHERRY TREE

(DULCIMER)

Old Joseph walked the mountain trail,
Young Mary struggled after.
Many a day had come and gone
Since she had heard his laughter.

Many a night had come and gone
Since she had seen her vision
And he had taken her away
From neighbors' sour derision.

"Don't straggle behind; we must get home
Before the sun goes down.
It ain't my fault your back is tired,"
Said Joseph with a frown.

They came upon a cherry tree,
Hung over a bank of mud
And filled to the top with ripest fruit
As red as any blood.

"Dear husband, hand me down, I pray,
One cherry from that twig.
I cannot reach it for myself
Because I am so big."

"What made you big was none of me,"
Groaned Joseph, looking wild.
"Let him hand down the cherry to you
That bigged you with the child."

Then came a voice from Mary's womb
Purer than any bird's.

It spoke upon the listening air
In clear commanding words.

"Bend down your branches, cherry dear,
Bend down your boughs, my brother;
Let your fruit fall into the lap
Of Mary, my little mother."

The branches knelt before the girl
To let her have her taste;
They rustled to her weary feet
And curved about her waist.

And Mary gathered to her heart
The words her baby said:
"Oh, Mother, do not grieve for me
To see me hanging dead.

"Out of the womb, beyond the tomb,
On Easter Day to rise,
A little while to wait for you
And greet you in the skies."

The branches rustled to the ground
To honor Heaven's queen.
Old Joseph had a shaking fit
At what he'd heard and seen.

"Oh, Mary, I have faulted you,
My dearest virgin wife.
Forgive me now and hear my vow
To serve you all my life."

"We both must serve the babe I carry
And wait for Easter Day.
Now, Mister Joseph, find me soon
A manger filled with hay."

Randall Jarrell

90 NORTH

At home, in my flannel gown, like a bear to its floe,
I clambered to bed; up the globe's impossible sides
I sailed all night—till at last, with my black beard,
My furs and my dogs, I stood at the northern pole.

There in the childish night my companions lay frozen,
The stiff furs knocked at my starveling throat,
And I gave my great sigh: the flakes came huddling,
Were they really my end? In the darkness I turned to my rest.

—Here, the flag snaps in the glare and silence
Of the unbroken ice. I stand here,
The dogs bark, my beard is black, and I stare
At the North Pole . . .
                    And now what? Why, go back.

Turn as I please, my step is to the south.
The world—my world spins on this final point
Of cold and wretchedness: all lines, all winds
End in this whirlpool I at last discover.

And it is meaningless. In the child's bed
After the night's voyage, in that warm world
Where people work and suffer for the end
That crowns the pain—in that Cloud-Cuckoo-Land

I reached my North and it had meaning.
Here at the actual pole of my existence,
Where all that I have done is meaningless,
Where I die or live by accident alone—

Where, living or dying, I am still alone;
Here where North, the night, the berg of death
Crowd me out of the ignorant darkness,
I see at last that all the knowledge

I wrung from the darkness—that the darkness flung me—
Is worthless as ignorance: nothing comes from nothing,
The darkness from the darkness. Pain comes from the darkness
And we call it wisdom. It is pain.

A PILOT FROM THE CARRIER

Strapped at the center of the blazing wheel,
His flesh ice-white against the shattered mask,
He tears at the easy clasp, his sobbing breaths
Misting the fresh blood lightening to flame,
Darkening to smoke; trapped there in pain
And fire and breathlessness, he struggles free
Into the sunlight of the upper sky—
And falls, a quiet bundle in the sky,
The miles to warmth, to air, to waking:
To the great flowering of his life, the hemisphere
That holds his dangling years. In its long slow sway
The world steadies and is almost still . . .
He is alone; and hangs in knowledge
Slight, separate, estranged: a lonely eye
Reading a child's first scrawl, the carrier's wake—
The traveling milk-like circle of a miss
Beside the plant-like genius of the smoke
That shades, on the little deck, the little blaze
Toy-like as the glitter of the wing-guns,
Shining as the fragile sun-marked plane
That grows to him, rubbed silver tipped with flame.

THE WOMAN AT THE WASHINGTON ZOO

The saris go by me from the embassies.

Cloth from the moon. Cloth from another planet.
They look back at the leopard like the leopard.

And I . . .
            this print of mine, that has kept its color
Alive through so many cleanings; this dull null
Navy I wear to work, and wear from work, and so
To my bed, so to my grave, with no
Complaints, no comment: neither from my chief,
The Deputy Chief Assistant, nor his chief—
Only I complain . . . this serviceable
Body that no sunlight dyes, no hand suffuses
But, dome-shadowed, withering among columns,
Wavy beneath fountains—small, far-off, shining
In the eyes of animals, these beings trapped
As I am trapped but not, themselves, the trap,
Aging, but without knowledge of their age,
Kept safe here, knowing not of death, for death—
Oh, bars of my own body, open, open!

The world goes by my cage and never sees me.
And there come not to me, as come to these,
The wild beasts, sparrows pecking the llamas' grain,
Pigeons settling on the bears' bread, buzzards
Tearing the meat the flies have clouded . . .
                      Vulture,
When you come for the white rat that the foxes left,
Take off the red helmet of your head, the black
Wings that have shadowed me, and step to me as man:
The wild brother at whose feet the white wolves fawn,
To whose hand of power the great lioness
Stalks, purring . . .
            You know what I was,
You see what I am: change me, change me!

FIELD AND FOREST

When you look down from the airplane you see lines,
Roads, ruts, braided into a net or web—
Where people go, what people do: the ways of life.

Heaven says to the farmer: "What's your field?"
And he answers: "Farming," with a field,
Or: "Dairy-farming," with a herd of cows.
They seem a boy's toy cows, seen from this high.

Seen from this high,
The fields have a terrible monotony.

But between the lighter patches there are dark ones.
A farmer is separated from a farmer
By what farmers have in common: forests,
Those dark things—what the fields were to begin with.
At night a fox comes out of the forest, eats his chickens.
At night the deer come out of the forest, eat his crops.

If he could he'd make farm out of all the forest,
But it isn't worth it: some of it's marsh, some rocks,
There are things there you couldn't get rid of
With a bulldozer, even—not with dynamite.
Besides, he likes it. He had a cave there, as a boy;
He hunts there now. It's a waste of land,
But it would be a waste of time, a waste of money,
To make it into anything but what it is.

At night, from the airplane, all you see is lights,
A few lights, the lights of houses, headlights,
And darkness. Somewhere below, beside a light,
The farmer, naked, takes out his false teeth:
He doesn't eat now. Takes off his spectacles:
He doesn't see now. Shuts his eyes.

If he were able to he'd shut his ears,
And as it is, he doesn't hear with them.
Plainly, he's taken out his tongue: he doesn't talk.
His arms and legs: at least, he doesn't move them.
They are knotted together, curled up, like a child's.
And after he has taken off the thoughts
It has taken him his life to learn,
He takes off, last of all, the world.

When you take off everything what's left? A wish,
A blind wish; and yet the wish isn't blind,
What the wish wants to see, it sees.

There in the middle of the forest is the cave
And there, curled up inside it, is the fox.

He stands looking at it.
Around him the fields are sleeping: the fields dream.
At night there are no more farmers, no more farms.
At night the fields dream, the fields *are* the forest.
The boy stands looking at the fox
As if, if he looked long enough—
                              he looks at it.
Or is it the fox that's looking at the boy?
The trees can't tell the two of them apart.

Lance Jeffers

WHEN I KNOW
THE POWER OF MY BLACK HAND

I do not know the power of my hand,
I do not know the power of my black hand.

I sit slumped in the conviction that I am powerless,
tolerate ceilings that make me bend.
My godly mind stoops, my ambition is crippled;
I do not know the power of my hand.

I see my children stunted,
my young men slaughtered,
I do not know the mighty power of my hand.

I see the power over my life and death in
another man's hands, and sometimes
I shake my woolly head and wonder:

    Lord have mercy! What would it be like . . . to be free?

But when I know the mighty power of my black hand
   I will snatch my freedom from the tyrant's mouth,
know the first taste of freedom on my eager tongue,
sing the miracle of freedom with all the force
   of my lungs,
christen my black land with exuberant creation,
stand independent in the hall of nations,
root submission and dependence from the soil of my soul
and pitch the monument of slavery from my back when
I know the mighty power of my hand!

William Keens

A PLACE BY THE RIVER

You take what it gives you, what a spinster
gave this farmhouse. Barren pear trees
remain of the land but the house
maintains itself with the life sunk into it,
seeming pious and generous
as the body of a sleeping saint.

Canning jars, calendars, a box of clothing,
letters, tracts, and Bibles: in each object
her presence gathers
as you distinguish the woman in her surroundings.
She was brief, God-fearing,
suspicious of dying, cautious, certain,
and sane. She kept Christ's picture
like a husband's or lover's
and a picture of Job articulating his pain.

In a room you lean by a window,
listening to a mockingbird in a pear tree.
You want to cup in your hands the voice like water
and drink or pour. A clear stream,
it winds mid-air from the limb through every room,
and you wonder if this was the tone of her strength;
if the keeper she kept within her whispered
in a voice so solitary.

You watch the bird, and in the distance between you
envision a winding, muddy river,
baptism by immersion and the glorious hysteria.

Ardis Kimzey

THEMES ON A VARIATION

Last night the dog
        moaned
beside the door.

The maple leaves
        jerked with the first
drops of iced rain.

The man beside me sighed,
        whispering in his sleep
a name that wasn't mine.

Said he'd dreamed a woman
        he had never seen
lay weeping in his arms.

On the ground this morning
a satin scarf snaked and curved,
        length enough to strangle

any summer.

Tom Kirby-Smith

HARVEY BEAUMONT'S COMPLAINT

Because she was not one to tease
A skein, until the ends come free,
I cannot solve my wit's amaze
Nor find out where I lost the way:
Here any turning will deceive.

And, though it was no practiced art,
I did not think a voice could weave
So strange a pattern, shift and dart
Quick as a shuttle darts, and leave
A woven brightness where it came.

What I saw has left me mad
With images I cannot name
Nor fix in tapestries, where clad
In gauze the Graces make a game
To weave the wind that lifts their hair—

Where delicate fingers reach to clutch
Bright tissues from the shifting air,
But fading at a second touch—
And so she caught me unaware
And bound me by her guileless craft.

One woman took a spider's shape
Because her fingers were too deft.
Another, while her suitors slept,
With greater cunning stripped the weft
And so did she: with wilful hands

Soon as the lifeless web of threads
Was figured through with vivid strands
She quick undid it: warp and woof
She plucked her labor into shreds
And raveled out the cloth she wove
Which was the fabric of my love.

Amon Liner

MORNING STROLL

Pleasant and cool
as the sky
on a dull morning,
I am at the intersection
with no roads leading away.
I hear the buzz of distant traffic,
the innocuous crumbling of the skyscrapers,
the humdrum final screams
of the people as they melt. Pleasant
as the stoplight
which is fixed on green
and is barely visible
against the pale sky of my cool,
I look at the weatherbeaten houses
for some sign of death,
but they stand venerable and smooth
as pleasantries,
as if they contained life,
although I know the living
have moved their furniture into storage.
Beyond my line of sight,
gas stations explode in impressionist
squeals of yellow and orange,
and people parts fly disconnected
through the crystalline air.
Gracious as a cool drink of water,
I stand at the end of the dusty path,
watching the rats crawl out into the road
and flop over and die
stoically. Just behind me I can see
myself, covered with long, damp green weeds,
scuttling through the soft fur

of my childhood, and just beyond range
of my hearing, some miles of the freeway
snap upward like a wounded ferret
and grind together, filling the meaty sky
with tenuous bits of concrete.
Pleasant and passable in the late morning,
I stand at the intersection, noting
the few things that really annoy me,
the absence of roads, and the
white obelisk, freshly painted but by some inexcusable
error, blank, with no names of streets
or any direction.

WITHIN THE INTERVAL

some write in a secluded place,
loud with flowers and water,
some write where lovers meet,
in cafes and in bed,
and some write from the place where I am
at the end of the world,

from which the sound depends,
as a grey-green bell
size of a child's head,
invisible.   In the air
of nonchalance,
the sound closes down
upon me, where I am,
at the end of the world,

where flowers grow,
grey as steel, brown as steel,

blue as steel, orange as steel,
vibrating in dirges and jingles
like any colors.   In the air
of surprise, sounds fade away
until only neutral tones
break my ears and I grow blind,
where I am, at the end of the world—

if there is such a place,
where grown knives circle in the air
and blood twists in huge, free-standing
columns, and eyes glitter
at every point.   In the air
of desolation, swinging
in the grey-green air, the child's head hollow
rings bell-like the sound
backward to shatter the clocks
at the end of the world—

as if there were never any other place to go,
and no other age to make the journey.
It is a kind of a comfort
to write at the end of the world,
a place where all the nuances of grey
have their Just harmony,
and the blood collapses into the concrete,
and the knives rust on the counter,
and the eyes fade into light,
as the bell rings because the bell rings
whatever the hour and even if no hour
is this place, where I am, at the end of the world.

Lou Lipsitz

THE NIGHT

Like old shadows,
highways of diseased moonlight—
like an ancient sore
torn out of the sky,
the night begins to enter us.

And within nerves there is a stirring of strange boots.
Silently, in the blackness, a rifleman
smelling of decay knocks on the door of his room
untouched since World War II.

On a dark stairway, a man stares into abandoned apartments
looking for his father's praise.
Slowly, the mind opens
and blood vessels reach out
like huge trees, touching the dark.

Alone.
Across the great distance of dreams
men cannot help each other.
And there is that silence—
as if a mute were dragged under by the sea.

TO A FIGHTER KILLED IN THE RING

In a gym in Spanish Harlem
boys with the eyes of starved leopards
flick jabs at your ghost
chained to a sandbag.

They smell in the air the brief truth of poverty
just as you once did:
                    "The weak don't get rich."

You made good.
Probably you were a bastard,
dreaming of running men down in a Cadillac
and tearing blouses off women.

And maybe in your dreams great black teeth
ran after you down dead-end alleyways
and the walls of your room
seemed about to collapse,
bringing with them a sky of garbage
and your father's leather strap.
And you sat up afraid you were dying
just as you had so many nights as a child.

Small bruises to the brain.
An accumulation
of years of being hit.

I will not forget that picture of you
hanging over the ropes, eyes closed,
completely wiped out.
Like a voice
lost in the racket of a subway train
roaring on under the tenements of Harlem.

COLD WATER

Cold water on my bare feet.
You are like cold water.

All day I've watched the water
run from the tap, splash into the bushes
where the earth awaits it
and sucks it up.

Cold water! The grass exclaims.

Norman Macleod

THANKSGIVING BEFORE NOVEMBER

The evening fire has gone up the chimney
To mingle with the anonymity of stars,
The dust of loneliness stirring the ashes
Over the Persian rug, the cradle
Of the easy chair: dispensary of comfort,
Ceased of rocking: come to a full
Stop like the interim of tomorrow
In the bedroom of my neighbor's wife.
There is torpidity of pain and worry
Over the grocery store across
The corner.   The towels of the bath
Are carefully arranged, the mat
Waiting: the coffee pot takes the image
Of a samovar for study at night.
The slow wind on the mire of the earth
Pokes questioningly at the strange
House of a man with no qualms.
Next Saturday the butcher's boy
And the query of icemen.   They change
So often the face of Nowadays.
It is hard to recognize an aunt
When she comes bearing cousins
To dinner upon Thanksgiving Day
And the slow querulous quest
Of the genealogy of fathers.

E. T. Malone, Jr.

POEM, FOR A GIRL WHOSE FULL NAME HAD
THE SAME NUMBER OF LETTERS AS DID MINE

These days, when I think
of Patricia,
I remember candy apples
and salt tears
with madness:
seven letters in one day,
driving with the top down
in the rain,
making love on a hardwood floor,
mysterious comings and goings
of body and of mind,
a shortwave radio signal
full of bleeps and squawks
without explanation
fading in and out,

out,

out.

Adrianne Marcus

A LAST DIALOGUE: MOSES

Father, I have gone through
Those seven places you call Faith
And I have managed.
Now age, particulars,
The cold exception of the wind
Hold me to this rock.
This Moab.
I did not crave this journey,
Others had more eloquence,
Longer faith. And when
You stretched a land before us,
A separate place of rumored
Milk and honey—I was afraid.

With plaques as thick as law,
We ran from Egypt, armies fast
Upon our heels, till there,
Collected by flat water,
We waited for the thick Red
Sea to group, to pass into
The wind, heard Pharaoh curse
And drown, his soldiers drown again.

Your word, my stone:
From that mountain I descended.

Saw your lion crouched
In ghettos
Whimper like disaster for a name,
A molten calf that damned us
Faithfully.

I split a kingdom
For our thirst—
No rock was worth that price!
Now you call me here
To bargain faith, to show me
Canaan, its green plains far
Below; the olives, fat and ripe
That shimmer from the trees.
Is heaven more than that?

I lean into mortality.

Harold Grier McCurdy

AT NOBSKA

Sea-tumble, under the sea-ploughing wind,
Green, blue, blue-green, amethyst, white,
Snow-snarl over the pig-backed rocks;
And the terns plunging; and the long, low hazy-finned
Blue islands, and the clear ascending height
Of the sky; and I, here where the surf knocks,

Contemplating—not, by any means, the face of man,
Or any work of man's, or any delight
Comprehensible by man, or any power
Within the control of man, no, but merely—a man's span
Of the infinite ingenuity of the supreme Light,
A jot of the Logos, a split-second of the towering

Billions of light-years of God's artifice!
Yet even the hairs of my head are numbered, and the fall
Of a single sparrow is noticed, and the diving tern
And the captured fish, and every blow and kiss,
Bounding or broken heart, slapped kelp, spray, star, all,
Inconceivably conceived by Him, are His minute concern.

A MOBILE

Wire and string
Comprise the thing:

Wire for bone
Of the skeleton,

String to serve
For the fine nerve.

More bodiliness
It scorns as excess.

String taut
With intense thought,

Wire bright
With abstract light,

It swings, swings,
In intelligent rings;

A species of grace
Vibrant in space.

Heather Ross Miller

THE CREMATION OF R. J.

We are not to think of Christ Church
where the poet, dead on his bier,
lay catnapping nine lives.

Upstairs on Fisher Park Circle,
we girls combed out our long bright tortoise locks,
snapping electricity,
curling,
purring to the lascivious comb.

Cheshire seasons dazzle me now,
so many cremations later,
the sunny-striped grass,
sycamores like orange explosion,
crisp,
cured,
tied off to stand in a shock and dry.

The Halloween candles return me to my flesh,
giving its light straight-out naked,
in a raw rind,
grinning—
        melted in the morning
        down to a
            formless
                babe.
I keep hearing the match rasp against my bones,
my hair goes up in a yellow corona,

and these eyes flare out.
I eclipse the moon,
each fingernail a fiery spear.

Cheshire,
see me grin.
Wake up and spin, nine lives.

GRANDMAMA JOCASTA

Unlucky queen,
the bulls running barefoot
through my early garden,
trampling the vine,
the purple bloom.

I smoothed my sidecombs,
and took a cup of tea,
to sit and think it out.

The slow swing of that steady cradle,
that china cup on a golden hook,
instructed me:

      the menfolks pitched this tent,
      bridged this starry flood,
      then welcomed me
      to the hive of comets, stinging meteors,
      they kept on leash.

But I got you, boy,
announced by birds, lambs, a god:
you threw yourself headlong,
trampling me.

I was your tame sweetheart,
I lived in your cage by day;
by night I wept and searched.

By night I searched for my crying boy,
crippled up, left to starve.

Empty cradle, empty swing,
each blossom struck off,
by the dumb barefoot:
                these are my harvests.

But I praise you,
little papilio, butterfly,
God will die home to supper,
and the killer limp to Thebes.

Jim Wayne Miller

ON NATIVE GROUND

This wind is blowing me all time's weathers,
mingling near and far, pennyrile
and woodsmoke, crow's call and carrion.
In a jay's harangue saws are singing; the swung
ax flashes in a lifting wave; twanging
still in a white-faced hornet's whine
a barbed-wire fence caught in a cuff once crossing.

Seed fallen in flesh rich as woodsdirt,
gone days spring up, trees from sown sweat.
Now is this green tree's growing bark, this always
was and is and forever tree-shading
summer was and is and summer will be.

A waterbead quivers on my hand:
there is a way to enter. Underfoot
a mole's nightwork gives way—O doors
are everywhere: the spring at the mountain's
foot holds the running taste of childhood,
the barking fox blurts the mountain's riddle.
Transparent minnows hanging in green water:
windows onto sunken summer days.
I enter through a fish's eye to one
vast room glowing in cold light.
Out of an oilspill on a rainslick road
campfires of a hundred hunts are blazing.
A dog's eye caught in headlights on a turn:
rose windows warm in his cathedral skull.
I travel everywhere on native ground;
roads turning into darkness turn me home,
plunge me into cool air of the mountains.

Gray marble monuments bending in a graveyard,
skewed reflections swaying on rolled water,
straighten to still gray chestnut stumps,
a chimney stack among old trees and roses
sprawling over tumbled corner stones
sprouting second growth. A new house rises.
Life grows in rings around a hurt,
a tree with barbed wire running through its heart.

THE BEE WOMAN

She carried the eggs in her straw hat and never
reached into a nest with her bare hand.
A woman who could conjure warts, who knew
charms for drawing fire, spells to make
butter come, and mysteries of bees
and hummingbirds, besides, knew to roll
eggs from a guinea's nest with a gooseneck hoe.

There is a mountain cove and light is leaving.
Speckled guineas fly to roost in trees,
their potterick and screech drifts far away,
becomes the faintest peeping in my dream
of stifling afternoons when we would stand,
the old woman and I, by fencerows and cowtrails
listening for half-wild guineas screeching
as they came off nests they'd stolen away
in thickets, briers, scrub pines, and chinquapins.

And no matter where I wake—horn's beep,
ship's bells, clatter of garbage cans,
strange tongues spoken on the street below,

in a rising falling bunk out at sea—
everywhere I stand on native ground.
The bee woman may pass through my dream:
running under a cloud of swarming bees,
she beats an empty pie pan with a spoon
till the swarm settles, black on a drooping pine bough
and guineas regroup pottericking—all
moving toward waking's waterfall.

SOWING SALT

This is a season of small miracles.
Dreamt from his rock by the barn, the fossil fish
swims in the light between barn roof and moon.
Scattered in the mountains, all my days
heave to their knees like cattle and come bawling
down from mountain pastures overnight,
starved for salt I sow over the rock.
I am restored. I salt the fish away.
Mother light licks me dry in a pasture.

Robert Morgan

TOPSOIL

Sun's heat collects in leaf crystals
crumbling.
Earth grinds the grain
to dark flour, drifts black flannel
over rock and clay.
Life invests
and draws on.
A lake rises over the world,
heaps of the rotting ocean.
Sun's heat adding
weight
piles on its light
century after century tarnishing
earth's metal.
Traffic of roots
hurrying. Places the raw meat
shows through torn to the quick.
Red clay mirrors.
Black fruit
growing around the earth, deepening
in the autumn
sun drifting down.

TOOLSHED

The sticky smell of rust breaking out in blisters
after every wet spell and burning hoeblades, plows,
crowds the eaves with dryness and wets the lower air.
Dust is stuck to the greased singletree.

Wasp nests like gray sunflowers
hang from tin. The air here hasn't moved
in thirty years, old snow hovering above ground.
Pale weeds grow to cracks.
Half-eaten shovels lean on plows
caked with forty-year-old mud.
Dust drifts crossed by snake zags. Broken clevis.
Plow points are nailed like rusting leaves
to the rafters. Dauber combs dripping plaster.
A bird looks out of its nest in the corner like a dragon
lurking. 1936 license plate,
hames sucked weightless by dry rot.

BEES AWATER

You find one drinking at the creek,
scratching and drinking
before take-off.
He lifts back
and takes aim, firing homeward.
That's the moment to get your sighting,
get the direction and slant of climb
and you'll be looking right at the tree
on the ridge above
where the honey hangs inside
like cells of a battery
charged with sweetness.
The whole tree has the hum of a transformer.
Bees bubble, circling
like electrons.

Though excited as before a holdup
and hot from the long climb,
you drop the ax
and wait for dark.

Paul Baker Newman

SKIMMERS

Where you see the undersides of their wings
the flock is white and flickering in the sunlight
above the sandbar and the blue water of the sound
and you can hear them crying and protesting
in the cool sea wind that blows across the channel,
and where the rest of them are turning toward you
they are all black and flickering in the sunlight
and they go swinging in a long Cartesian figure
like a twisted plane that lets you see its outlines
by its colors, the one half white and tilting away,
and the other half black and tilting toward you,
as they swing into the air and call you all the names
they can think of in the time it takes to rise
and get away, loping on their long black wings
so leisurely toward the sound behind the islands.

WASHINGTON AND THE APES

Touring the San Francisco Zoo
I watch the movements of animals, their lack of plan.
It is important to do things new.

Washington might have felt so
watching a gorilla family roll
like barrels in the dusty hold

of a Barbados rum ship he had sailed.
Cracking nuts and joking by the hour
he must have felt no particular desire

to call himself the great white ape
rolling like a hogshead with his kind
across the playful continent,

or to substitute Jamaica grog
for his particular wine. But made it do
at the officers' table in seventy-nine.

I love these images.
Washington at his table. The gorillas
in their zoo, wild wolves behind him.

Man is an aimless animal.
That gave him a plan. To stay between
the British and the mountains,

his flanks extended by the forest,
his communications open to the rivers,
his rear protected by the animals.

NOTE: *Early in the Revolution Washington realized that he must never let the British get between him and the mountains. His role was to outlast the British, with nature as his ally.*

JULY FOURTH WEATHER

The night wind
comes with its rain of salt,
a ripple of green blue-berried cedar
sighing through the wind's teeth.
Steel grey the inlet widens
beyond the shoals, dark-
ening and turning silver,
long restless lines of break-
ers wash the dark grey sand
with overlapping planes of
cloudy silver, where the sea oats
nod their harsh plaited seeds.

Guy Owen

FOR JAMES
(1926–1965)

May there be basketballs in Beulah
and you bouncing arpeggios
looping in rainbow arcs
under hosannas of saints.

Let there be hunting in heaven, too
persimmons with possums dangling like fruit
and under your calm bead
bucks bearing trees of lightning
to fall in pools of painless blood
rising over and over.

I wish you basketballs and deer, James
you who left our hearts
like old leather   unlaced
unfit for game or chase.

MY FATHER'S CURSE

My father strode in anvil boots
     Across the fields he cursed;
His iron fingers bruised the shoots
     Of green, he stabbed the earth.

My father cursed both sun and rain;
     His sweep cut corn and weed,
And where his fiery plow had lain
     The ruined earth would bleed.

Yet though he raged in bitter brew
     Thick oaths that belled his throat,
God rammed His springing juices through
     And fleshed Himself in fruit.

Reynolds Price

ANGEL

Every angel from its height
Sheds a pure though blinding light,
Intermittent noon and night.
Yet—or therefore—it deserves
Thanks, attentions, steady loves:
Every angel on its height
Burns itself, itself its light.
Burn, clear angel—I observe,
Thank, attend, attempt to serve.

Sam Ragan

THAT SUMMER

That summer when the creeks all dried up
Except for a few deep holes
Under the caved-out roots of oaks
Now leaning toward the water's edge.
The catfish clung to the mud
But now and then a perch was caught
In the oatsack seine.
Even the Tar was a trickle
And I could walk all the way across
On the rocks, and the place
Where we had swung from limb to water—
Splashing below surface and rising sputtering
Was now no more than moist mud
From which a turtle crawled.
> They sat on the porches
> And talked of the weather,
> And Herbert Hoover,
> Cursing both, and every son of a bitch
> Who had voted for him.
> Even if the Baptists saved any souls
> Worth the saving
> Where in the hell would they find the water
> To baptize them.
A wild turkey flew out of the woods
And even if it was out of season
He fed a family for two days.
And it was better than that mud turtle
That looked like mud and tasted like mud . . .
> that summer when it didn't rain.

"THE PROPHET"

He has grown quieter now,
And almost forgotten—
The Prophet
Only comes to town at tobacco-market time,
And he's only moved to preach
When pimply-faced boys snicker
At his long grey beard and high black hat.
He'll roar at them then,
Damnation and spittle directed at their faces.

But there was a time—yes, there was a time—
When they would not have laughed.
There was a time when he stood in the street
With eyes lifted to an August sun
And hellfire pouring from his lips,
Throwing their sins out for all to see.
The poor bastards who felt that hell could be no hotter
Than the tobacco rows down which they marched—
But sin was real and damnation sure,
And the Prophet knew where to hit them where it hurt.
He could preach for an hour, two hours, and they would listen,
Scuffing the dirt and never hunting shade
Until the Prophet had poured out his scorn
And walked away.

The old man's fire is gone now.
He dozes in the shade of a mulberry tree
And mumbles to himself, brushing flies from his face—
Hell is far away,
Beyond the cornfield, the cotton patch,
And maybe even beyond the dusty towns of long ago.

FLANNERY O'CONNOR

. . . the peacocks cry all night long: help me, help me.

Four miles from Milledgeville on a farm
Of five hundred acres
She raised chickens (and peacocks).

She talked of grotesques,
Southern style—of freaks who felt
The call to preach,
Of praying violent men with something
In the blood driving them
Onward but inward.

Broiler prices had been falling,
And it had not rained for weeks.
The grass was almost gone in the pastures.
There had been a fire,
But the damage was slight.

She held their attention
With strong Georgia phrases
Drawing pictures of a people
In a land all their own, shifting
Suddenly from darkness to hard sunlight,
Caught in the giant hands of fate and the will of God.
        But the violent bear it away.
        And a good man is hard to find.

The crutches lean against the wall
Unnoticed and forgotten.
In the shade of the trees
The peacocks strut.

        But at night in the mellow darkness
        They cry . . .
        All night long . . .
        Help me.
        Help me.

T. J. Reddy

BLACK CHILDREN VISIT MODERN JAIL

From this cage
I see Black children pass in the halls
I see their eyes absorbed
In steel paneled concrete corridors

I hear them told by jailers
How modern this facility is
I see them shown guards and control towers
That regulate doors
I see them shown cameras that scan,
Microphones that hear the sounds
That cry out inside this can

Let me tell you, Blackchildren,
These robotized followers of rules
Won't let you see why we are here
They won't let you see children your age
Caged here with me
They won't let you hear the screams
Or see the bloodstained floors
They won't let you understand
Why 85% of those caged here
Are Black bodies like mine, like yours

Black children visit modern jail
Hurriedly they move along in a line
Huddled close side by side
Can they see they too are caged
Can they see themselves captives
Of classrooms learning ignorance
Can they see themselves captured
By American lies?

Black children I can see
How "criminal" you are forced to be
For stepping out of line to be free
From the lies
Like me

Campbell Reeves

THE DAPPLED PONIES

When dappled ponies gobbled roses from the hedges
and cobwebs hung spread-eagled from the wires
dew-clotted innocent of victim bait or spider

When morning ran the mists out of the valley
and all the little suns were coming up at once
        over the mountain

Then I remember steam from kneeling cattle
rising in mushroom puffs above their heads
the fierce horns the sweet and holy haloes
the heavy beasts all born again
        reincarnated saints

Saint Angus and Saint Brahmin a bull
named Gabriel rose like a martyr a wreath
of tenderness around his head
        and knelt again sighing

Saints live long but dew is swift in drying

If grace is sought I think about the valley
nurturing its nectarines and honey
the ponies nibbling roses from the hedges

The dappled ponies with their saddles squeaking

Dannye Romine

PRIMER ON DIGGING

*Memory is the characteristic art form
of those who have just decided to die
and those who have just decided to live.*
—Daniel Stern
The Suicide Academy

Listen: when you dig
in the garden
expect to be bitten.
Those fish heads you buried
last spring endure beyond seasons,
breeding their own subtleties.
Your fingers will encounter
the slow growth of moss,
the spasms of slugs
recoiling from salt.
Go further: one mild earthworm
is not sufficient to measure the world.
Hard by the brick wall
the roly-poly unfurls,
a bolus of damp memory
assaulting your nostrils.
Wait. Don't reach for the spade.
You must touch the white root
with your fingers, follow
its search for cool water.
Now that your hands are submerged
notice how the dark treasures
quicken like dreams
beneath your swollen fingertips.

Gibbons Ruark

`A PROGRAM FOR SURVIVAL

When what we thought was a distant star has fallen
And hums in the last of the fields beyond the last
Of the cities, we must approach it from a new
Direction. Descending from the rooftops, leaving
The helicopters idling in their harnesses,
Peeling off the gas masks and instruments of torture,
Let us walk into the country through the morning
Darkness. Somewhere on the way let each of us
Pause and hang his clothes on the branch of a fallen
Tree. When we come together into the clearing,
Let us form a ring of glowing human bodies
Around the monstrous flying thing from another
Planet that throbs and bristles with a thousand arms.
By the light that strikes us from its fascinated
Windows, we will see our enemies and neighbors
Fleeced with a dozen shades of body hair, their pale
Genitals unfolding delicate as tendrils
Or tucking under them like smiles. Let us lie down
With our lovers when we know them, falling on them
Softly as possible, rocking with them, getting
Up and turning to the future humming in the grass.
As the salt of loving glistens on our bodies,
Let us admire ourselves in the mirroring surface
While the machine is gentled and admires us all.

FINDING THE PISTOL

Dragging a rake through layers of my sleep
Blown down like leaves in a dream of weather,
I haul to light as through a developing water
Something the child has never seen before,
Though she knows it clearly for a kind of weapon.
It is a snub-nosed pistol, gray and scabbed with rust
The color of blood or the leaves that covered it.
She fondles it and turns it over in her hand
Until I see it batten on her knuckle
Like a damaged finger and she cannot let it go.
She aims it at me out of every bush
And I can hear the hammer clicking like a shutter.
Someone is taking a picture of me.
It comes up smoking through the leaves of water
And smiles down at me from my father's gallery.
I never saw till now the thing I nestled in my hand
And pointed like a finger at the camera.
I never knew before who took the photograph,
Who lost a heartbeat when he heard the hammer fall,
As it will no more than once or twice in our
Overlapping lives, on an empty chamber.

Roger Sauls

DREAMING OF MY MOTHER

Wake up cold.
Drape the tartan blanket around my shoulders
And watch the early sky
Heal away the stars.

In the secondary growth
The leaves of young elms
Have completely turned.
They blow in the wind
Like a tree of yellow butterflies.

Winter must mean death.
If I went back now I'd find
The dry fields
Plowed under, sown with rye and
Oats, the shirts on the clothesline
Stunned by cold.

My mother was small
And all her life she grew smaller.

Tonight I saw her in a dream,
A white body rising
From water like a surprised bird.

From her sickbed she heard her children singing.

I think of her now only
At night, when I am deep
In the forgetfulness of dark.

In her hospital gown she was white as the
Sand roads she walked, small as the dust.

When she died I was wandering in a dream.

I drove my car down every street I knew,
The pale sky drilled with stars.

DIARY OF A MADWOMAN

after a photograph by Rosamond Wolff Purcell

My name is Helga. My hair is the color
Of Swedish linen, pulled back into a knot
The size of a McIntosh apple. I walk barefoot
Among the leaves, even though there is no sun,
And the grass is as still as a dry broom.

I think today it will rain. The parsnips
Will grow another inch into the ground, and
I can imagine lying down under there among
The knots of their delicate root system, as if
I were surrounded by spiders.

As a girl I left a chair out in the rain.
Afterward I wanted to take it apart
And leave it, like a description of my mind.
I wanted a strand of pearls to circle my neck
Twice, and make an island of my head.

Still, I can feel the light on my body
As I stand here, arms poised like wings,
And the high stone wall behind me cracking
Into large sections of calm.

James Seay

IT ALL COMES TOGETHER
OUTSIDE THE RESTROOM IN HOGANSVILLE

It was the hole for looking in
only I looked out
in daylight that broadened
as I brought my eye closer.
First there was a '55 Chevy
shaved and decked like old times
but waiting on high-jacker shocks.
Then a sign that said J. D. Hines Garage.
In J. D.'s door was an empty Plymouth
with the windows down and the radio on.
A black woman was singing in Detroit
in a voice that brushed against the face
like the scarf
turning up in the wrong suitcase
long ago after everything came to grief.
What was inside we can only imagine—
men I guess trying to figure what would make it
work again. Beyond them
beyond the cracked engine blocks and thrown pistons
beyond that failed restroom
etched with our acids beyond that American Oil Station
beyond the oil on the ground
the mobile homes all over Hogansville
beyond our longing
all Georgia was green.

I'd had two for the road
a cheap enough thrill
and I wanted to think
I could take only what aroused me.
The interstate to Atlanta was wide open.
I wanted a different life.
So did J. D. Hines. So did the voice on the radio.
So did the man or woman
who made the hole in the window.
The way it works is this:
we devote ourselves to an image
we can't live with and try to kill
anything that suggests it could be otherwise.

Sharon Shaw

WE KNOW THE WORLD CAN TURN

We know the world can turn,
in a thousand ways shift beneath us.
And we know this is no explorer's land
where stars, flights of birds,
seaward-drifting wood promise land.
For when our stars rise, the earth vanishes,
sinks beneath its own horizon
when the birds depart. And the drifting wood
drifts from shores that never
existed at all.

        And so, bereft of mariner's signs,
you concentrate on some crazy tiny thing—
the sound of rain—and catch,
if only for a moment,
your human balance in the mist of waiting
for another turn, a new sound.

FOR LEONARD WOOLF

The summerhouse
gathers to itself
remnants of a world.
Here upon the grass a walking stick,
a ribboned summer hat
upon this desperate grass
green-struggling to the in-lapping water.
Fixed center now of nowhere: the stick,
the hat,
the still
unopened envelope.
Astonishingly dry now all
these remnants,
all
the world.

D. Newton Smith

MORPHE

You'd think I'd committed rape
the way she acts sometimes.
So what if I told her how it was—
how everywhere I looked
there they were, lounging, leaning
against some thing,
sitting on walls, or on the grass,
their naked arms, and bare brown legs
in short skirts, moving through
the quick of me in the breeze
that tossed and made their cloth
cling to bodies that were not real,
yet. Until I came along, that is,
and touched them with my hands,
and gave the truth to forms they had
but had not known, with palms they
hadn't known until they knew by touch.
Like when it took a tooth to tell a coin
there's something about the genuine
that wants a touch,
and touched becomes itself.

We were walking through a sculpture
garden once and I embarrassed her
by touching stone while someone
in a uniform looked, and came, and said,
"Please don't touch the sculpture."
He pointed to the signs that all but said
sculpture is nothing but painting in the round
and only for the eyes and not the hand.

But she understood, then,
that my delight confirmed my appetite—
for her, for form in stone;
they were both the shape of my desire.

Desire, I said—and it
just raises all hell with her . . .
When all I did was try
to tell the feeling of the wind,
to share the reality of the touch
that never was,
or was,
but only in my mind,
and now has need to be.

William Sprunt

SCARECROW

Peg-leg actor
Hung with night
Why are you hopping
Largo into my city
Go back
Among your white stalks

Your cross bones
Hold no meat
Your cape
Does not breathe

You are no thing
But the absence of crows

NEWTON ON ANOTHER DAY

Here is no senseless gravity
This is force:
To wring sweat from stones
Swell tides of blood
Open caves of origin
Turn years in upon themselves
Build mansions from painted rooms
Make evenings festivals.

Smelling of apples and Eve
You wait in your taut skin.

Something lengthens in the grass.

Thad Stem, Jr.

CRISIS

An old man leading his jackknife horse
Around the fringe of darkening woods,
Mumbling about the accursed wilt
And wild grass running as ravenously
As a gang of vampires.

The season's terrible, crops are worse,
And idiot papers speak of dark troubles
Somewhere off beyond the horizon.
Trouble is it! By God, they ought
To tangle awhile with downy mildew
That kisses young plants with the lips
Of the devil, himself.

Wonder what's for supper now?
A rasher of fine, lean side meat?
He clucks to his horses excitedly—
Flying sparks from steel on stone
Send fireflies sailing to Settle's Lane.

SCHOOL DAYS

He knew he had the place alone
And he'd better find out who was puttering
Around the wood pile and singing such
A sad, sad song.

It was only the wind out there
Playing a made-up game of bloodhound,

Sniffing the chips and fallen leaves,
A forgotten child playing by himself,
Poking through the hedgerows just to see
How the other side would look.

For all the apple green was gone,
And all the blue and pink and gold, and
The wind being left alone had to improvise.
You know, like a five-year-old in early Fall
When everyone's gone to school.

Shelby Stephenson

JANUARY HOG-KILLING

In water boiling every early January
just-shot hogs turn over in chain-traces
horizontal across the vat
after the twenty-two's balling the forehead
WHOMP firm shoat-meat falling
dead-on putting the world out
right between the eyes.
The jar passed round into draughts,
hootch made in some radiator
abandoned for rot-gut booze,
rising beads
bubbling
down in crackling fire,
ice-edged beams dripping
hot running blood of hogs,
gambreled,
puddling into thawing first-month earth.

Kathryn Stripling

INSOMNIA

That was no moment
I should spend this whole night asking
questions of. More like the moonlight merely
taking shape there on the ragged quilt
so that my fingers, touching it,
began to trace the stitches of another pattern's
tree of life's leaves branching like a peacock tail.
Or so it seemed that night I woke to feel

my grandmother living like my own skin
at that very instant feeling cold
wind from a broken window pane: no help
at all those scraps of calico she'd sewn together
for my birthday. It was too much
to be borne at twenty-two, the thought
of how her body must be sleeping
with its legs drawn up into themselves to hide
the toenails twisted like the true-love knots
she used to sew across the edges of her nightgown
sleeves. How could I dare to look
into her open mouth that breathed, that

breathed? At last a dog barked
blocks away and I got up to fetch a cigarette
to keep from hearing what I thought
must be her life's time passing like the sound
of bobbin thread unwinding, or the breath
from some collapsing lung. Or was it
my own life I was afraid to hear instead,
its blood-roots weaving me a gift
of silence too far down to comprehend?

CONTINUUM

Those who have slept
their lives long underneath these trees
and by day
move among them as quietly as dust
down the ladders of light,
looking up at the peaks
of them, the jagged patterns
treetops make against the sky
and through them the cut of a hawk's wing,
the curve of the river
of cloud shapes, these people

will dream of them
shifting like silt in the creek-bed,
or quartz as it heaves
in the earth's slow migration of seasons.

Their voices
will make of this turning
a music to echo their vision,

and likewise
their fingers will praise its existence
on bearhide and stone in a sundance
of spectrum, will take
every movement the wind gives
to water and weaving
it into their baskets and beadwork
will leave it to the sure waste of time
and the people who, like us,
come after them, having forgotten

that such a design
as my Waxing Moon Sister
Marina has seen beneath museum glass

and for three hours copied on paper
to transfer to fabric in stitches
so small she can't see them
and so must be led by the touch of the thread
toiling under her fingers
is forest itself, all
the forms of it translated into this fingerwork
through which the first sign is given
that says to us: See

and so make of it
something.

Julie Suk

A COLD CHUNK OF STAR

such a cold chunk of star slung into space

no wonder I sleep so close
pulling you into my curve
your mouth to my breast

a moon still warm
throbbing
throwing out light

your pulse in my flesh

our whole night is spent
hanging on edge
darkness pushing us out

no wonder we drift

the slow motion of feathers
settling in a windless house

all our lives are spun on collapse
sucked through a rip so black
we fling to the ground and hold

one hand tethered
the other snapping at dark

as we listen
for the light crackling out
the voice sent back still warm

Chuck Sullivan

THE GOING RATE

Flickering down
by the torches
the dawn shadows
shape-up in the slim
first light of another
working day

Bound in the free
enterprise of hired
hands holding their ground
in the still dark
marketplace of America

straw-hatted
overalled souls
chained to making
the early morning deal
with the bosses
who chant the call
of all they're worth
in the piecework
world of the going rate

While at the gate
the condemned
school buses wait
to roll the chosen
into the green pastures
of non-union alleys

where under the migrant sun
they bend their lives

to the slim pickings
of the crop rooted
beneath the company-blue
sky that Lords itself above
the going rate of the Imperial Valley

Charleen Swansea

RAP

The women's liberation news
Has set my mind to looking back.
Why did I believe that to give you the best
Was the best I could do?
Why have I spent so many years
In a weather watch on your mood,
Growing your seeds and seeding your clouds?
Dear John, this is just to let you know
That this and that about us disgusts me.
Our life is a game for half a mind,
The plays described by you for me.
Why did I believe that flowers sent
On special days could compensate
For cruel nights?
I stayed at home to send you out
In laundered shirts and polished shoes,
But I have time for looking back.
What if I had not thought I was pregnant
Or if you had not asked me to prove
My love for you; or if I had known
Some honest trade and someone to trust me,
Would we have married, would I be a slave
To my body, its alleys and halls?
Would I see the rules
Written wide as a wall?

Thomas N. Walters

SETON'S FOLKS IN DENIM FOUND
AMONG CONETOE'S FIRST

ugly   as hardshell   riverbank   sin
they trucked themselves   their things
lumped as   homemade soup   brownashy grit
their satchels   of   salvationish   junk
a potatoskinned   youngun   army   onto
Seton's farm   that   shining   Sunday

Rufus and Rosadene   were who
sharecroppers   their possum backbones clung to
with bigeyed   mooning   girls
moving slow   as their mother   bruised boys
raising   rocks   through forever air   around
trees   long   after birdsflight   were what

moving   and out   of season   along   at that
thumbing deeper   down   through   gut thin dimes

the rifleless pickup   borrowed   onceblue
bucked furrows   briars   to toss   cheap chairs
taped   and twined   pasteboard boxes from A&P
as if some timekeeper's   bell   might chime
a kerosene stove   scarring   painted steel beds
ammoniac mattresses abloom   with   circleyellows

we heard their kindling cut
smelled   chitterlings and tarpaper smoke
then   sounds to scare   cats   inside out
and   they were gone through   frosted fennel
squeezed between Marchwinds   and   The Man
cold mornings   creeping   at their heels

Robert Watson

THE RADIO ASTRONOMER

A radio astronomer in Utah lifts his ears
Over the moon and stars, sets them at empty space.
It's 3 A.M., a quiet hour. Beneath the moon it snows.

He sets his tape recorder to the ears, takes a coffee break,
Looks out the door at unintelligible random snow,
Its soft sound, drifting, each flake gorgeous as a number

In flight, gorgeous as stars and planets, their slow sounds
From long ago, cries amplified of stars in flight,
Sounds of the dead, the untranslatable tongues

Of the universe, where life other than this may be
Or was, surely, somewhere among the galaxies a signal
Could he hear it, in some recess a sound of familiar life.

Again he listens: the sounds seem random, or does he hear
A wheel turning, the click of dice, noise of cards dealt out?
A casino in the heavens? The powers wagering there?

He listens, tries to tie furniture of our lives
To each separate sound, sound to sight. The dice fall again.
The roulette wheel spins, slows, stops on an invisible number.

These sounds bring no grand music, no vision that Milton
Or Michelangelo knew. He unwraps a sandwich,
Pours more coffee. The sounds, he thinks, are random:

This is a universe of luck and chance. Galaxies
Spin in flight like snow, rattle in space, are gone.
For a while light lives, sound lives

Spinning through valleys and mountains of empty space:
God in sound, the great gambler sending in flight
The dice, the stars, the snow at 4 A.M. in Utah.

At 5 A.M. home through snow in bed he touches the breast
Of a galaxy, hears the dance of the heart and the lungs,
Feels the cells gather and shower, his children waking.

The sun explodes in the bedroom. The universe
Is gone: He falls to a soundless sleep, a corpse.

GOING NOWHERE ALONE AT NIGHT

All houses stand in pools of black.
A police car's blue roof-eye trails
Me down this Fall night of drifting
Leaves. I drift. I drift. It's wrong
To fall in love so many times,
So many times. The yellow leaves
This Fall more beautiful than last.

They curb me with a siren cry.
"Destination? Your license please!"
"Nowhere. I can't sleep." O the stars
Warm, luminous as . . . It's wrong
With half-dressed trees so lovely now
As you and they were and all are.
The blue light spins away in leaves.

Why don't I root myself in bed;
A black tree in rows, unmoving,
Of black trees? It's wrong to fall in love
So many times, so many times.

PLANET EIGHT

We clambered down in airtight suits to the ground
Of Planet Eight where the temperature
For us was cold. The sky was green and windless,
Our feet sank into dust that felt like fur.

We marched toward mounds and tall stones we thought
Must be a town, marched through a plain of dust
Where nothing grew, no tracks of bird or beast.
Under the layer of dust was a crust

Of rock. Our mallets tapped the house-high mounds.
We bored holes. Our gloves rubbed dust from walls of stone.
We found no sign of doors, no carved words.
A light flashed from our capsule, then our phone

Clicked with orders to return. That was all
I saw on Planet Eight, that stillbirth
Or corpse: we would have welcomed rats or flies.
But on the long weightless flight back to earth

With my life's high point shrinking to star size,
I dwell on the dust, the stone mounds, a life
Without life. I land on our stranger planet:
I look out with hostile eyes.

Marvin Weaver

LOST COLONY

They passed the pop bottle between them
at arm's length as if it were a calumet
black hair smoked their faces as they breathed
and twisted over upon their sides
and twitched their legs like insects

three of them there under the bridge
Simon Locklear, Willie Sampson, Rudolph Oxendine
Tuscarora, Lumbee, Croatan
whose old chiefs ate the first white spirits
beached behind the cape on Roanoke

rendered the medicine in their blood
who drank the strong mixture
half paint thinner half mountain dew
they called smoke-on-the-water
for reasons that ceased to matter.

John Foster West

BUZZARD'S KNOB

Jake Mitchell swore he didn't believe
in no god nor nothing you could point
your bony finger at, by God;
said he wanted to be buried on the tip top
of Buzzard's Knob among the green trees.
Said to wrap his carcass in an army blanket
and haul it there on a sourwood sled
pulled by a yoke of yearling bulls
lugging balls heavy as bell clappers.
Well, old Jake died like folks have
time and time again
and his old woman honored his druthers
to a frog-hair T.
And his bones slept in peace up there
among the green oaks and pines.
One day twenty years or so later on
I drove by Buzzard's Knob and stared at it.
The top had been lopped off down a ways
and a marble-gilded Baptist church
shining like a Hollywood motel
sparkled against the blue June sky.
Where old Jake made his mistake was
he didn't say how long to leave his bones
unbothered on the hilltop used to be his.

Jonathan Williams

DEALER'S CHOICE AND THE DEALER SHUFFLES
(for William Burroughs)

I saw the Chattahoochee River get a haircut.
I saw Fidel Castro flow softly towards Apalachicola, Florida.

I saw a bank of red clay integrate with Jesuits.
I saw Bob Jones Bible University used to make baked flamingos.

I saw the Governor of Mississippi join the NAACP.
I saw a black gum tree refuse to leaf and go to jail.

I saw the DAR singing *"We Shall Overcome!"*
I saw Werner von Braun knitting gray (and brown) socks
      for the National Guard.

I saw the Motto of Alabama: "IT'S TOO WET TO PLOUGH!"
I saw God tell Adam: "WE DARE DEFEND OUR RIGHTS!"

I saw the City of Albany fried in deep fat.
I saw eight catfish star on Gomorrah TV.

I saw "THE INVASION OF THE BODY-SNATCHERS" at the
      Tyger Drive-In.
I saw William Blake grow like a virus in the sun.

I saw the South suckin hind titty.
I saw the North suckin hind titty.

I saw a man who saw these too
And said though strange they were all true.

Postface:
'There was a crow sat on a clod—
And now I've finished my sermon, thank God.'

THE FLOWER-HUNTER IN THE FIELDS

(for Agnes Arber)

a flame azalea, mayapple, maple, thornapple
plantation

a white cloud in the eye
of a white horse

a field of bluets moving
below the black suit
of William Bartram

bluets, or "Quaker Ladies," or some say
"Innocence"

bluets and the blue of gentians and
Philadelphia blue laws!

high hills,

stone cold
sober

as October

Bartram's name to the Seminole was "Puc-Puggy," the Flow-
er-Hunter. He remains one of the very few great men to have
visited the Florida Lotophagoi since Cabeza de Vaca. . . . I am
most indebted to Mrs. Arber for the two books of hers I
know: Herbals *and* The Mind and the Eye (*both Cambridge*).

FOR GEORGE LEWIS (1952)

the way he said it
                (you knew it was the only way to say it)
: yessir, Ol George, he's the greatest!

and that's the way the One-Eyed Babe spoke it
as he heard the LP,
and held his worn bass bow so lightly in his grayed black hand

I'd passed right by him, he was squatting out of the sun
on Bourbon Street

his wife Jeannette, stood in the sun outside Musicians' Union,
told me:
                probably went right by him
                he was sitting over by his sister's place

the way she said it:
his position
                (like it was a kind of ceremony, a thing he took with him)
out of the daytime's drainage
through New Orleans

into the dark—
there, where it was
nothing but miracle
                        brought down from where it flies
                        by a battered clarinet,
                        by the prayers in this stick,
                        pointed into the heart of
                        a man

and there was nothing else anywhere
                                    to us,
                                    to this man,
     except the solitary magics in the wood
                         within his hand
     so he rode it, soared it up and down, around the heart of
     Slow Drag's bass
                    (backed by the banjo Marrero stuck)

               sung it in his blood
               held it in his arms

               shut his eyes to, was a man to—

                         was a god!

Emily Herring Wilson

BALANCING ON STONES

Perhaps the light bending
    in the wheat
or the pale undersides of
    summer leaves
filled up the old silences
    between us.
We found our way easy,
    across small streams,
walking in field daisies,
    naming birds.

Then we came to the place
    no human talk
makes sound without pushing
    beyond the limits
to where pain lies, dark
    as the creek banks,
pushing from a darker source,
    washing upon us,
adrift, frightened, quick,
    balancing on stones.

J. S. Winkler

HUNT

persimmon weather again and
the hounds of thirty years ago
bugle on hill and through hollow

Dal, or whichever midnight coffee man,
rousing nudges the age-grimed
pot back on the embers

myth or fox: predetermined winner—
hark to the race, swig with cronies,
cling in heart's heart to the frosting earth

persimmon weather again and someone you knew,
were, the ghost in the ruined dog trot,
stirs, whispers in the dusk

Biographical Notes

BETTY ADCOCK did not move to North Carolina until she was married, but her career as a writer began in the state. In the last decade she has served as an editor of *Southern Poetry Review*, participated in the Poetry-in-the-Schools Program, and read her poems on many college and high school campuses. She has also taught creative writing at Duke University. Although many of her poems spring from her Texas childhood, North Carolina has provided the impetus and background for much of her recent work. As she says, "The countryside around Raleigh is much like the east Texas landscape. . . . Besides, I love the ocean for itself and our mountains have a way of getting into my poems."

Betty Adcock was born in San Augustine, Texas, and graduated from Hockaday School. Although quick to call herself a college dropout, she has studied at four different colleges and universities. She has also worked as a copywriter for an advertising agency but recently resigned to become a full-time writer. She is married to Donald Adcock, associate director of music at North Carolina State University, and they have a daughter, Sylvia. Her poems have appeared in numerous national publications, including *Poetry Southwest* and *The Nation*, and she has won a number of important literary awards. Her first collection, *Walking Out*, was published in 1975.

A. R. AMMONS has been, since the death of Randall Jarrell, the state's most distinguished and influential poet. Author of twelve books of poetry, he has won the Levinson Prize and the Bollingen Prize; in 1973 he won the National Book Award for his *Collected Poems*. He has also served as poetry editor for *The Nation*.

Ammons was born near Whiteville, North Carolina, in 1926. His early years on a tobacco and cotton farm account for the pastoral setting of some of his most memorable work, as well as his poems about mules, hog-killings, hunting, and farmhands. At Wake Forest College, where he earned his B.S., his major interest was science, and much of the uniqueness of his style comes from his scientific diction. After a few months of graduate school he became principal of Hatteras Elementary School for a year and absorbed the sights and sounds of the Outer Banks. Later he became a business executive in New Jersey.

Since 1964 he has been a member of the faculty at Cornell University. He is married and has one son.

Ammons began writing during the long hours aboard ship when he was in the navy in the South Pacific. His first poems were influenced by his reading of Walt Whitman and Dr. William Carlos Williams. Generally opting for free forms, he has been concerned with man's relationship to nature (his favorite subject is a solitary walk in a rural setting of North Carolina or New Jersey), the problems of identity, permanence and change, and the processes of nature. Among his best books are *Expressions at Sea Level*, *Corsons Inlet: A Book of Poems*, and *Collected Poems: 1951–1971*.

JAMES APPLEWHITE was born in Stantonsburg, in Wilson County, and received his B.A. and M.A. from Duke University, studying under William Blackburn. After a teaching stint at the University of North Carolina at Greensboro, he returned to his alma mater to complete his Ph.D. and to teach creative writing and courses in modern poetry. He lives in Durham with his wife Janis and their three children.

While teaching at the University of North Carolina at Greensboro, Applewhite began publishing in regional literary journals. He had the good fortune to work under the informal guidance of Randall Jarrell and Allen Tate. Among his influences he has listed James Dickey, Theodore Roethke, and T. S. Eliot. He writes that Wordsworth and Whitman taught him "to admit folk characters into my poems in as whole form as possible." As is true of many Tar Heel poets, place is important in his work. His strongest, most authentic poems are rooted in the people and landscapes of Wilson County. Not surprisingly, one of his main themes is how the past of early attitudes and early memories impinges upon the present. Though he continues to work with folk characters and folk speech, his latest poems seem more literary in content and style than his early work dealing with the places and people of his rural childhood. His first collection, *Statues of the Grass*, was published in 1975.

DAPHNE ATHAS, a North Carolinian with a Greek heritage, was born in Cambridge, Massachusetts, and moved to Chapel Hill in 1939. She received her B.A. from the University of North Carolina at Chapel Hill and did graduate work at the Harvard School of Education. In the 1950s she lived in England, where she worked as Service Club Director for the U.S. Air Force. Primarily a writer of fiction, Miss Athas has published three novels, including *Entering Ephesus,* which won the Sir Walter Raleigh Award in 1972. She has lived and traveled extensively in Greece and has written about her experiences in *Greek by Prejudice.* Her stories, essays, and poems have appeared in numerous magazines, including *New World Writing* and *Transatlantic Review.* She is currently teaching courses in creative writing and contemporary literature at the University of North Carolina at Chapel Hill.

JAMES BARDON grew up in Alabama but has lived since 1970 in North Carolina. He graduated from the University of Alabama and received his M.F.A. at the University of North Carolina at Greensboro, where he studied with Robert Watson and Fred Chappell. His poems have appeared in over a dozen magazines, including *Shenandoah, The Little Review,* and *The International Poetry Review.* He is currently completing his first volume while teaching in a community college.

GERALD BARRAX is one of North Carolina's best-known black poets. Never a prolific writer, he has stressed control and an assured craftsmanship in his poetry. Although Barrax has pursued an academic career, as his poems testify, his experiences have been varied. He has worked as a steel-mill laborer, cab driver, mail carrier, as well as teacher. He also served four years in the air force and was stationed in the Philippine Islands. Born in Alabama, he spent ten years there before his family moved to Pittsburgh. He received his B.A. from Duquesne University in 1962 and his M.A. from the University of Pittsburgh in 1967. He then came to teach at North Carolina State University, where his areas of specialty are black studies and creative writing.

Of his move from the North to North Carolina, he writes, "I am certain that living here for the past decade is responsible for the increase in nature imagery in my work—i.e., the deliberate, conscious use of natural imagery." Barrax's poems have appeared in numerous black journals and anthologies of black writers, as well as in *Poetry* and *Southern Poetry Review.* In 1970 the University of Pittsburgh Press published his first book, *Another Kind of Rain.*

SUSAN BARTELS was born in Rice Lake, Wisconsin, in 1942, but lived in Charlotte, North Carolina, for several years, where she earned an M.A. in English at the University of North Carolina there. She is divorced and has one child. At present she is an instructor in the Department of English at Winthrop College while completing her doctorate at the University of South Carolina. Her poems have appeared in a number of magazines, among them *The Nation, Paris Review*, and *South Carolina Review*. Her first book of poems, *Step Carefully in Night Grass*, was published by John F. Blair in 1974.

RONALD H. BAYES was born in Freewater, Oregon, but has served as writer-in-residence at St. Andrews Presbyterian College for nearly a decade. He received his B.S. and M.S. degrees from Eastern Oregon State College and studied abroad in Ireland and Canada. An accomplished translator, he has lived and worked in Japan and Iceland. Since coming to North Carolina, Bayes has directed the N. C. Poetry Circuit and founded both *St. Andrews Review* and The Curveship Press. He has also published numerous critical articles on such modern writers as Ezra Pound and Yukio Mishima. He lists Dr. William Carlos Williams and Charles Olson as important influences. Among his recent books of poetry are *King of August* and *The Casketmaker*, which won the Roanoke-Chowan Award.

JOHN BEECHER is by nature and heritage a poet of protest. A relative of Henry Ward Beecher and Harriet Beecher Stowe, he has expressed with the same strong voice his concerns for America and the destiny of her people. Many of his poems deal with the injustices suffered by the poor, both black and white. Beecher was born in New York City in 1904, but at the time he began writing poetry, he was working in the steel mills of Alabama. He received his B.A. from the University of Alabama and his M.A. from the University of Wisconsin; he also studied at several other universities, including the University of North Carolina at Chapel Hill. In the twenties and thirties he was an English instructor and then a government administrator. During World War II he served in the U.S. Maritime Service and was awarded a Combat Medal. Since then he has been, among other things, administrator of a displaced persons camp, sociology professor, rancher, printing press operator, poet-in-residence at various colleges and universities, and journalist. Married and the father of five children, he has now retired to Burnsville, North Carolina.

Beecher began writing in the 1920s because he felt impelled to speak out about the exploitation and suffering of steel-mill workers. During the 1930s he wrote about the unemployed, the migrant workers, the sharecroppers, and other victims of the Great Depression. In the 1940s he wrote about injustice in the United States against a background of a war for freedom abroad. In the 1950s he wrote also about the denial of civil liberties; in the 1960s he wrote of the civil rights movement. His poems look back to Whitman in their romantic faith in America's possibilities and in their compassion for the American common man, but in subject matter they have been addressed to the concerns of the immediate present. He has published eight books of poetry, and his *Collected Poems, 1924–1974* covers fifty years of his poetic war against oppression.

HELEN BEVINGTON was born and reared in upper New York State; however, her active career as a writer began when her late husband joined the faculty at Duke University. She has lived in North Carolina since 1943, and many of her five hundred poems reflect life in the state. Two of her collections have won the Roanoke-Chowan Award. Mrs. Bevington grew up as an only child in a Methodist parsonage. After graduating from high school, she received her Ph.B. from the University of Chicago and her M.A. from Columbia University. She has worked as an editor and teacher, and for over three decades taught courses in writing at Duke University. She is also the mother of two sons.

After moving from New York City to the country near Durham, Helen Bevington began writing poetry in 1945 because "of the particular pleasure of living in the country." Her career was launched when she won a contest conducted by Houghton Mifflin. The following year she published her first collection, *Doctor Johnson's Waterfall*. She is best known for light poems that are witty and polished and marked by a disciplined grace. Her themes often come from her wide reading, her extensive travels in Europe, or the landscapes and lifestyles observed in North Carolina. Although she refuses to take herself seriously as a poet, her poems often strike a somber note. As Richard Walser has observed, "[B]eneath the excellent good taste and exuberance, a skillful intelligence is seriously at work." Among Helen Bevington's most popular collections are *A Change of Sky; When Found, Make a Verse Of;* and *Beautiful, Lofty People.*

CHRISTOPHER BROOKHOUSE was born in Ohio in 1938 and, before moving to North Carolina, lived in California and Massachusetts. Currently he teaches creative writing and modern literature at the University of North Carolina at Chapel Hill. He writes, "I live deep in the woods of Chatham County among deer, owls, copperheads, and a rare bobcat. I like the silence of the South, for I think poetry is silence, that the words one struggles to find and shape into a whole leave a silence around the heart, a silence rare and pure which can be heartbreaking." In addition to a novel, *Running Out*, he has published two collections of poems, *Scattered Light* and *If Lost, Return.*

FRED CHAPPELL was born in Canton, North Carolina, and earned his B.A. and M.A. degrees at Duke University, where he studied under William Blackburn. He now lives in Greensboro with his wife Susan and son Heath. He is professor of English at the University of North Carolina at Greensboro, teaching in the writing program.

Chappell has written four novels, the most recent being *The Gaudy Place*, and two books of poetry, both of which won the Roanoke-Chowan Award. His latest collection, *River*, is organized around images of water: a river, floods, his grandfather's baptism, and a well-cleaning task which is like a drowning and rebirth. His subjects have ranged from baseball and pornographic films to science fiction to a satellite and beyond. All his novels, short stories, and poems are set in North Carolina, and he finds himself tied to the state by "deep affection and angry impatience." He has written, "It's a marvelous state to write in, considering the landscape and the multiplicity of speech patterns. Hardest thing is to write about it as it is *now*: in transition from nineteenth-century rural to twentieth-century ruination."

ANN DEAGON was born and reared in Birmingham, Alabama, but she has spent her entire career as a poet in North Carolina. She did not begin writing until she was forty years old, when "that three-headed dog love death and poetry/took me in its teeth and shook me." Since 1970 she has been one of the most prolific poets in the state; she has published nearly two hundred poems in over fifty different magazines. Her four collections are *Poetics South, Carbon 14, Indian Summer,* and *There Is No Balm in Birmingham.*

Upon graduation from Birmingham Southern College in 1950, Deagon enrolled in the graduate school of the University of North Carolina at Chapel Hill, where her great-great-grandfather had been an undergraduate. After receiving her M.A. and Ph.D. in classics, she joined the faculty of Guilford College. She now lives in Greensboro with her husband Donald and their two daughters, Andrea and Ellen.

It is easy to detect a Southern voice behind many of her poems: she is a born storyteller, and she is drawn to a Southern landscape, often employing folk motifs and folk speech. On the other hand, many of her poems might be called academic, springing from her wide knowledge of classical myths and literature and her travels in Greece and Italy. This is especially true of the poems in *Carbon 14.* Her major theme is love; as she writes, "That's what everything else turns into for me."

HARRIET DOAR recently retired as book-page editor for the *Charlotte Observer* and now devotes herself to writing full time. She attended Duke University and the University of North Carolina as a special student. While pursuing an active career in journalism, she managed to publish both fiction and poetry. Her poems have appeared in *Red Clay Reader, The New York Times,* and *Southern Poetry Review;* she has also been anthologized in *Eleven Charlotte Poets* and *North Carolina Poetry: The Seventies.*

CHARLES EDWARD EATON was born in Winston-Salem, where his father was mayor for many years. After graduating from the University of North Carolina at Chapel Hill, he studied philosophy at Princeton University, then took his M.A. in English at Harvard University, where he studied under Robert Frost. In addition to teaching courses in literature and writing in Puerto Rico and at the University of Missouri, he served as vice-consul at the American embassy in Rio de Janeiro for four years. His stay in Brazil resulted in a collection of stories, *Write Me from Rio.* Upon returning to this country, he was for five years in charge of the creative writing program at the University of North Carolina. Currently he is a full-time writer, living half the year at Chapel Hill and half in Woodbury, Connecticut. He is married to the former Isabel Patterson, and they are both avid collectors of American paintings. His hobbies are art, music, gardening, and swimming—all of which have influenced his poetry.

Among North Carolina poets with a national reputation, Eaton is probably the most classical in style. He has been praised for the manner in which he has been innovative while still utilizing traditional verse patterns. Robert Graves and Conrad Aiken, among others, have commented on the "Southernness" of his work. Widely published in periodicals here and abroad, Eaton is the author of a book of art criticism, six books of poetry, and two volumes of short stories. Two of his recent collections of poetry are *Countermoves* and *On the Edge of the Knife*, which won the Roanoke-Chowan Award. In 1974 his *The Man in the Green Chair* won the Alice Fay di Castagnola Award of $3500, which is given by the Poetry Society of America for a work-in-progress. Recordings of his poems are in the collections of Yale University and the Library of Congress.

JULIA FIELDS has lived in North Carolina for more than ten years, though she was born and grew up in Alabama. A graduate of Knoxville College, she studied at Bread Loaf and the University of Edinburgh and received her M.A. from the University of Connecticut. In addition to teaching in New York and Alabama, she has taught in a number of North Carolina colleges, including East Carolina University, St. Augustine's College, and North Carolina State University. She has two young daughters. Julia Fields is the author of a number of short stories and plays, and her poems have appeared in numerous national magazines and anthologies. Her two books of poetry are *Poems* and *East of Moonlight*.

ROBERT WATERS GREY was born in Olney, Maryland, but has taught at the University of North Carolina at Charlotte since 1969. He graduated from Brown University with a degree in history and received his M.A. from the University of Virginia; his thesis was a collection of original poems. Grey is married and has one son. His poetry has appeared in over a dozen journals and anthologies, and he was awarded the Academy of American Poets Prize at the University of Virginia. With Nancy Stone he co-edited an anthology of contemporary Southern poetry entitled *White Trash*. He is assuming the editorship of *Southern Poetry Review*. Among his recreations he lists "ransacking old buildings and dreaming of owning a horse."

O. B. HARDISON, JR., director of the Folger Shakespeare Library in Washington, D. C., has lived in North Carolina for long periods of time and plans to return to the state when he retires. Born in San Diego, California, he earned two degrees from the University of North Carolina at Chapel Hill and received his Ph.D. from the University of Wisconsin in 1956. He is married and the father of six children. While on the faculty at the University of North Carolina at Chapel Hill, he was recognized by *Time* as one of the country's outstanding educators. He has a national reputation as a Renaissance and medieval scholar and is the author of two collections of poetry, *Lyrics and Elegies* and *Pro Musica Antiqua*.

WILLIAM HARMON was born in Concord, North Carolina, in 1938. After earning a B.A. at the University of Chicago, he joined the navy and spent seven years on active duty assigned to a destroyer. He has lived in Hawaii, Japan, Northern Ireland, and South Vietnam. In 1970 he returned to North Carolina, with a Ph.D. from the University of Cincinnati, to teach at the University of North Carolina at Chapel Hill. He remains a Lieutenant Commander in the U.S. Naval Reserve. He is married to the former Lynn Chadwell and has a son and a daughter.

"I used to wish (and once in a while pretend)," he writes, "that I came from some very *Southern* kind of South: the picturesque peasantry of the mountains, say, with feuds and moonshine and all that; or else the sweetly decayed aristocracy of the lowlands, with colonelcies and juleps and all that. But, after seven years in the Midwest and seven years in the Navy, I came home again (it's easy) to be another sort of Southerner, not a very Southern one. Most Harmons work in cotton mills."

Harmon is the author of three books of poetry, including *Treasury Holiday* and *The Intussusception of Miss Mary America*. He specializes in humorous verse written in an informal and conversational style, and for satirical poems he often chooses topical material drawn from news items and American politics. His hobby is anthropology, which provides the material for many of his poems. He has also published articles on contemporary poetry and has edited *The Oxford Book of American Light Verse*, which will appear in 1979.

LODWICK HARTLEY was for several decades a professor of English and head of the English department at North Carolina State University. He has published six scholarly books and numerous articles in critical journals. His poetry and short stories have appeared in *Sewanee Review, Georgia Review, South Carolina Review, Southern Humanities Review, Southern Poetry Review,* and *University Review,* among others. His latest work is a fictional memoir entitled *Plum Tree Lane.*

THOMAS HEFFERNAN, of Irish descent, has spent much time in Ireland, but has lived in North Carolina since 1971. He earned his M.A. from Boston College and pursued further graduate work in Perugia, Italy, and the University of Manchester, England. He has recently been director of the North Carolina Poetry-in-the-Schools Program and has edited a number of anthologies of student poetry. His poems have appeared in numerous regional journals, including *Crucible, St. Andrews Review,* and *Tar River Poets.* His first collection, *Mobiles and Other Poems,* was published by St. Andrews College Press in 1974.

GILL HOLLAND, born in 1936 in Lynch, Kentucky, has been on the faculty at Davidson College since 1961. He received his B.A. from Washington and Lee University and his Ph.D. from the University of North Carolina at Chapel Hill. He is married and has three children. In addition to publishing poems and stories in a number of regional magazines, he has won the Mishima Prize for fiction offered by *St. Andrews Review* and the Sam Ragan Prize for poetry sponsored by *Crucible.* He has also been active as a translator of Chinese poetry.

FRANCIS PLEDGER HULME was born in Hawthorne, Florida, in 1909, but moved to Asheville when he was three years old. He attended both Duke University and the University of North Carolina at Chapel Hill, later earning his doctorate at the University of Minnesota. Now semi-retired, he has been employed as a teacher, violinist, and music and drama critic. In addition to writing, he raises fancy bantams and collects Royal Doulton dogs and Hiroshige prints. At present he is teaching a course about North Carolina writers at Warren Wilson College. Hulme has published many poems making use of the traditional forms and folk idioms of the Appalachian mountains. His two collections are *Come Up the Valley* and *Mountain Measure*.

RANDALL JARRELL when he died in 1965 was North Carolina's most famous poet. He was also one of the nation's most distinguished men of letters, active as teacher, editor, critic, novelist, and translator. He served as literary editor of *The Nation* and poetry critic for *Partisan Review* and *Yale Review*. In 1956–58 he was Consultant in Poetry to the Library of Congress. Among his numerous honors and awards were a National Institute of Arts and Letters grant and the National Book Award. He was the most influential literary figure of his generation in the South.

Jarrell was born in 1914 in Nashville, Tennessee, but spent much of his childhood in California. He graduated from Vanderbilt with a B.S. in psychology and later earned his M.A. in English, studying poetry with John Crowe Ransom. During the war he spent four years in the Army Air Corps, serving as a Celestial Navigation tower operator. Out of his war experiences came some of his most powerful poems, collected in two volumes that made him famous as a war poet, *Little Friend, Little Friend* and *Losses*. In 1947 he joined the faculty at Woman's College in Greensboro, where he taught creative writing and modern literature. Among his many books are *The Woman at the Washington Zoo*, *The Lost World: New Poems*, and *The Complete Poems*. Two recent critical studies are *Randall Jarrell, 1914–1965* edited by Robert Lowell, Peter Taylor, and Robert Penn Warren and *The Poetry of Randall Jarrell* by Suzanne Ferguson.

LANCE JEFFERS was born in Fremont, Nebraska, in 1919, but has taught creative writing and black literature at North Carolina State University for six years. He graduated *cum laude* from Columbia University, where he also received his M.A. He has taught at Tuskegee Institute, Howard University, and California State College in Long

Beach. Jeffers is married and the father of two daughters. His poems, stories, and articles have appeared in numerous national magazines and anthologies, including *The Best American Short Stories* and *Nine Black Poets*. His two collections of poetry are *My Blackness Is the Beauty of This Land* and *When I Know the Power of My Black Hand*. He is also a jazz pianist.

WILLIAM KEENS, born in 1948 in New York City, grew up in Reidsville, North Carolina. He received his B.A. from the University of North Carolina at Greensboro and his M.F.A. from the Writers Workshop of the University of Iowa. He currently teaches English and creative writing at Ravenscroft School in Raleigh. His poetry has appeared in a number of journals, including *American Review, Malahat Review,* and *Southern Poetry Review*. In 1977 Penumbra Press published a chapbook of his poems entitled *Dear Anyone*.

ARDIS KIMZEY was born and grew up in Washington, North Carolina, and received her B.A. from Duke University with a major in sociology. She is married to a Raleigh lawyer and has three sons. Her poems and reviews have appeared in a number of regional magazines, including *Red Clay Reader* and *Pembroke Magazine*. She currently reviews children's books for the Raleigh *News and Observer*. Having been director of the state's Poetry-in-the-Schools Program, she has edited anthologies of student poems and written a book on the program in North Carolina.

TOM KIRBY-SMITH has been, since 1967, on the faculty of the University of North Carolina at Greensboro, where he teaches creative writing and edits *The Greensboro Review*. He also teaches astronomy and has published a book entitled *U.S. Observatories*. A graduate of the University of the South, he studied at the universities of Paris and Dijon as a Fulbright Scholar, as well as at Harvard and Stanford, where he was a Poetry Fellow. His poems and translations have appeared in numerous journals, including *Sewanee Review, Virginia Quarterly Review,* and *Hudson Review*.

AMON LINER, from Charlotte, North Carolina, was born in 1940 and did his undergraduate work at Catawba College and Kenyon College. Later he took an M.A. in drama at the University of North Carolina at Chapel Hill and in 1976 an M.F.A. in creative writing at the University of North Carolina at Greensboro. His poetry has been published in a number of regional magazines, and his first collection, *Marstower*, was issued by Red Clay Books. For years a victim of ill health, Liner died in 1976. *Chrome Grass: Poems of Love and Burial* appeared posthumously.

LOU LIPSITZ, like most of North Carolina's poets with a national reputation, is a college teacher. Surprisingly, though, he does not teach English; he is a professor in the Department of Political Science at the University of North Carolina at Chapel Hill. He generally avoids the literary themes and allusions that are the hallmark of many academic poets.

Lipsitz is an adopted Tar Heel, having been born in Brooklyn, where he grew up and graduated from high school. After earning his B.A. at the University of Chicago, he earned two graduate degrees at Yale. In addition to teaching, he has worked as a journalist. He is also the editor of *American Politics: Behavior and Controversy*. He was married in 1959 and is the father of two children. Moving to North Carolina has had a discernible influence on the poet's work; the varied landscapes of the state appear in his most recent poems. His first collection, *Cold Water*, was published in 1967.

NORMAN MACLEOD, born in Salem, Oregon, in 1906, has been a professor of English at Pembroke University for the last decade. He received his B.A. from the University of New Mexico and his M.A. from Columbia University. He has taught in numerous American schools and colleges, as well as in Mexico and Canada, and worked as a journalist and editor in Holland and the USSR. Widely known as a founder and editor of literary magazines, Macleod has also published two novels and four collections of poetry, most recently *Selected Poems of Norman Macleod*. He is poet-in-residence at Pembroke State University, where he edits *Pembroke Magazine*. In 1975 he won the Horace Gregory Award for his contribution to American letters.

E. T. MALONE, JR., was born in Wilson, North Carolina, and received his B.S. from Campbell College and his M.A. from the University of North Carolina at Chapel Hill. He is married and has a daughter. He has worked as a journalist and illustrator and has recently been assistant city editor of the *Durham Sun*. Among his hobbies are gardening and etching. His poetry has appeared in such regional journals as *Tar River Poets, Crucible*, and *The Lyricist*. In 1972 his *Tapestry Maker* was published by John F. Blair.

ADRIANNE MARCUS was born in Everett, Massachusetts, but grew up in Fayetteville, North Carolina. She attended Campbell College and the University of North Carolina at Greensboro, where she studied under Randall Jarrell. She received her M.A. from San Francisco State University and is currently a part-time instructor at the College of Marin in Kentfield, California. Mrs. Marcus is the mother of three children. Her poems have appeared in numerous national publications, including *Atlantic Monthly, Paris Review*, and *The Nation*. In addition to a book on photojournalism, she has published a chapbook of poems, *The Moon Is a Marrying Eye*.

HAROLD GRIER MCCURDY was born in Salisbury, North Carolina. He received his doctorate from Duke University in 1938 and has taught biology, psychology, and philosophy. He is now Kenan Professor of Psychology Emeritus at the University of North Carolina at Chapel Hill, where he lives with his wife Mary. Since retiring he is learning to play the piano "in the eternal hope of being resurrected in the company of Bach." His poems have appeared in *The New Yorker* and *Prairie Schooner*, as well as in regional poetry magazines and anthologies. The modern poets who have influenced his work are Eliot, Yeats, and Frost. His collection of poems, *The Chastening of Narcissus*, was published in 1970.

HEATHER ROSS MILLER was born in Albemarle, North Carolina, in 1939. She earned a B.A. and M.F.A. at the University of North Carolina at Greensboro, where she studied under Randall Jarrell. She is married and the mother of two children. She lives in Badin and is an instructor in English at Stanly Technical Institute. Born into a writing family, she has written poetry, short stories, and novels and has published seven books, including the novels *Gone a Hundred Miles* and *Tenants of the House*; a book of short stories, *A Spiritual Divorce*; and two books of poetry, *A Wind Southerly* and *Horse, Horse, Tyger, Tyger*. Her latest project is a nonfiction book which combines folklore and nature.

JIM WAYNE MILLER was born in Leicester, North Carolina, where he graduated from high school. Later he received his B.A. from Berea College and his Ph.D. in German and American literature from Vanderbilt University. At present he is a professor in the language department at Western Kentucky University at Bowling Green. He is married and has three children. Although he no longer resides in the state, his parents and five brothers and sisters still live in the mountains of North Carolina.

Miller began writing poetry and stories as a first or second grader, imitating the writers he enjoyed reading. Later, when he began writing seriously, he came under the influence of Robert Frost and Edgar Lee Masters, as well as the modern German poets. He has also written ballads in the tradition of the ancient songs he learned as a boy in the North Carolina mountains, where much of his work is rooted. His major themes are the relationship of the living to the dead and the persistence of past experience. In his most recent poems he has moved away from subjective themes to expressing the collective life of the Appalachian region, its past and future. His two collections are *Copper Head Cane* and *Dialogue with a Dead Man*.

ROBERT MORGAN was born in Hendersonville, North Carolina, and from 1944 until 1961 lived in Zirconia, which provided the background and themes for his early poems. He graduated from the University of North Carolina at Chapel Hill in 1965, later receiving his M.F.A. from the University of North Carolina at Greensboro. At present he teaches creative writing at Cornell University. He is married and has two children.

Robert Morgan has plowed and harvested crops, and his poems about the joys and hardships of life on a mountain farm clearly spring from "felt experience." He aims "through structures and discoveries of language . . . to exalt the humble and ordinary, to show that the ordinary is really the extraordinary." Since moving away from North Carolina Morgan has written poetry centered more directly on the mountains and people of his childhood. His latest work depends less on imagery alone and more on a plain style combined with a narrative center. His poetry has been collected in three volumes: *Zirconia Poems, Red Owl,* and *Land Diving.*

PAUL BAKER NEWMAN, a latecomer to North Carolina, has achieved an important place in the state's literary scene. Drawn to the Carolina coast by his interest in sailing, he has written many poems with a coastal setting; other poems are about the nature and landscape of the state, as well as its history.

Paul Newman was born and grew up in Chicago, Illinois. He earned his M.F.A. at the Writers Workshop at the University of Iowa and his doctorate at the University of Chicago. After teaching at Manhattan, Kansas, he joined the faculty at Queens College, where he teaches creative writing. He lives in Charlotte with his wife Ann, and they have three children. In addition to his academic career, Newman has worked as a weather forecaster and served five years in the army during World War II. As his poems reflect, in the last decade he has traveled all over America and much of Western Europe; recent poems have been set in Italy, Greece, and Ireland.

In the 1970s Newman became interested in integrating poetry with film-making. He made a film based on his book-length poem about his daughter Paula and another based on a sequence of poems on George Washington, which was written for the Bicentennial. He has published over two hundred poems in magazines and anthologies. His five collections are *The Cheetah and the Fountain, Dust of the Sun, The Ladder of Love, Paula,* and *The House on the Saco.* He has twice won the Roanoke-Chowan Award.

GUY OWEN was born in Clarkton, North Carolina, in 1925, and holds three degrees from the University of North Carolina at Chapel Hill. He has taught at Davidson College and Elon College and served as writer-in-residence at the University of North Carolina at Greensboro and Appalachian State University. At present he is professor of English at North Carolina State University, where he teaches creative writing and has edited *Southern Poetry Review* and *North Carolina Folklore Journal*. Owen is the author of four books of fiction, including *Journey for Joedel* and *The Ballad of the Flim-Flam Man*, and two collections of poetry. *The White Stallion and Other Poems* won the Roanoke-Chowan Award in 1969. With Mary C. Williams, he co-edited *New Southern Poets* and *Southern Poetry: The Seventies*. His hobbies are reading and listening to a wide range of music.

REYNOLDS PRICE was born in Macon, North Carolina, in 1933. He graduated *summa cum laude* from Duke University and was a Rhodes Scholar at Oxford University. Currently a professor of English at Duke University, he has served as writer-in-residence at the University of North Carolina at Chapel Hill and other universities. Among his numerous awards are the William Faulkner Foundation Award, the Lillian Smith Award, and a Guggenheim Fellowship. His poems have appeared in a number of journals, including *Shenandoah*; his widely acclaimed works of fiction include *A Long and Happy Life*, *A Generous Man*, and, most recently, *The Surface of Earth*. He is now working on a translation of passages from the Bible.

SAM RAGAN has been so busy pursuing a number of careers and promoting other writers that one wonders when he finds time to write his own poems. Although he is primarily a journalist, he has also been active as a television commentator and moderator, critic, editor, and teacher of writing workshops. In his widely read column "Southern Accent," begun in the Raleigh *News and Observer* in 1948, he has discovered and encouraged many young poets who later made important contributions to the state's literature.

Sam Ragan was born in Berea in Granville County and except for serving in the army in the Pacific during World War II and working on a Texas newspaper, he has lived in North Carolina. After graduating from Atlantic Christian College, he edited weekly papers in Moore and Onslow counties and worked as a journalist in Wilmington, Goldsboro, and Concord. After the war he moved to Raleigh, where he became executive editor of the *News and Observer*. He is now editor and publisher of *The Pilot* in Southern Pines, where he lives with his wife Marjorie. They have two daughters. In his poems Ragan writes of the "relationship of man to his world, the natural world and the man-made world," and there is a suggestion of Robert Frost in his treatment of rural scenes and people. His two collections are *The Tree in the Far Pasture*, winner of the Roanoke-Chowan Award, and *To the Water's Edge*.

T. J. REDDY, born in Savannah, Georgia, in 1945, has lived in North Carolina for more than ten years. After attending Johnson C. Smith University, he did graduate work at the University of North Carolina at Charlotte. He was project director for the Community Center in Charlotte, where he also edited the literary magazine *Aim* and worked as a reporter for the *Charlotte Observer*. His poems have appeared in a number of magazines and anthologies, including *Red Clay Reader* and *A Galaxy of Black Writing*. A member of the Charlotte Five, who were convicted of burning a riding stable, he has published *Less Than a Score, But a Point*, a collection of poems growing out of his prison experience.

CAMPBELL REEVES was born and educated in Auckland, New Zealand, but has lived in Raleigh since 1946. She is married to an architect and has two sons. She has been active in promoting the arts in North Carolina, has taught in the Poetry-in-the-Schools Program, and has served as president of the North Carolina Poetry Society. Her current project is establishing a new art gallery. Her poems have appeared in over a dozen literary magazines and anthologies, and she has published two collections, *Bane of Jewels* and *Coming Out Even*, which won the Roanoke-Chowan Award in 1974.

DANNYE ROMINE was born in Miami, Florida, in 1941, and educated at Florida State University. Since 1963 she has lived in North Carolina. A teacher, writer, editor, and translator, she has taught in the Poetry-in-the-Schools Program and is presently book editor of the *Charlotte Observer*. She began writing in a creative writing course taught by Phillips Russell at the University of North Carolina in Chapel Hill. Besides her poetry, which has been published in such journals as *Paris Review* and *Carolina Quarterly*, she has written short stories and a history of Charlotte's downtown area. She is married and has two sons.

GIBBONS RUARK was born in Raleigh in 1941 and educated at the University of North Carolina at Chapel Hill and the University of Massachusetts, where he received his M.A. He has taught at the University of North Carolina at Greensboro and is currently at the University of Delaware. He lives in Newark, Delaware, with his wife and two daughters. His poems have appeared in *The New Yorker*, *Poetry,* and *Southern Poetry Review;* and his first collection, *A Program for Survival*, was published in 1969. His latest book is *Reeds.*

ROGER SAULS was born in Lowndes County, Georgia, in 1944, but has spent much of his adult life in North Carolina. A college dropout, he has worked as a publisher's representative and a clerk in a bookstore. For the past six years he has lived in Chapel Hill with his wife Caroline and son Brian. He has given many readings throughout the state, and his poems have appeared in *Kayak, Southern Poetry Review, Carolina Quarterly,* and other poetry journals. Loom Press in Chapel Hill published his *Light* in 1975.

JAMES SEAY was born in Panola County, Mississippi. After graduating from the University of Mississippi, he earned his M.A. at the University of Virginia in 1966. He is currently teaching at the University of North Carolina at Chapel Hill. He is married and has two sons. As his poems testify, he is a dedicated fisherman and hunter. His poems have appeared in numerous magazines, including *American Review* and *The Nation.* He has published two collections in the Wesleyan Poetry Series, *Let Not Your Hart* and *Water Tables.*

SHARON SHAW came to North Carolina in 1963 to teach at East Carolina University. Born in Columbus, Ohio, in 1937, she earned her B.A. at Ohio State University and her M.A. at Purdue. She has lived in Pakistan, Greece, and Canada, as well as Colorado, Indiana, and New York, but has settled down permanently in North Carolina and now teaches English at Sandhills Community College. Her poems, which she says are her "attempt to get a handle on the world," have appeared in a number of journals, and she has been featured poet in an issue of *Tar River Poets.* She is also the author of several critical studies of modern poets. John F. Blair published her *Auctions* in 1977.

D. NEWTON SMITH was born in Duncan, South Carolina, in 1939, and was educated at the University of North Carolina at Chapel Hill. He received his Ph.D. in 1974, writing a dissertation on the origins of Black Mountain poetry. He was a founder of *Lillabulero*, a literary journal, and has taught at the University of North Carolina at Chapel Hill and Western Carolina University. He is married and the father of two sons and currently works as a free-lance writer and publications consultant. Smith's poetry has appeared in over a dozen Southern journals, and he has published a chapbook entitled *15 Poems*.

WILLIAM SPRUNT is a radiologist who began publishing poetry in the 1970s. Although he was born in Shanghai, China, he was educated in North Carolina. After majoring in English at Davidson College, he went to the Harvard Medical School, returning to Raleigh to practice. He began writing in the 1960s and studied three years with Caroline Kizer at the University of North Carolina at Chapel Hill. His poems have appeared in such magazines as *Southern Poetry Review*, *St. Andrews Review*, and *The Nation*. His *Sacrifice of Dogs* was published in 1977.

THAD STEM, JR., might be called the dean of North Carolina letters. A regionalist in the best sense of the word, he has been content to spend almost his entire life in his native Oxford, living on the same street where he was born, writing about his hometown and state. Poetry, he says, "is the real aim and objective of my life," and since 1944 he has written and published an astonishing number of poems. In addition he has written history, biography, fiction, and criticism. For many years he has been an editorial writer for the Raleigh *News and Observer*, while also writing a syndicated column of humor. His journalistic style is characterized by his light touch, his wide knowledge of books and history, and his love of nature. In addition he has been generous with his time in encouraging young Tar Heel writers, both as an informal guide and as a reviewer.

Following his graduation from Duke University, Stem served in the army during World War II. After the war he worked as a Veterans Service Officer in Greenville. In 1947 he married Marguerite L. Anderson, a portrait painter and teacher. Besides his varied career as one of the state's most active writers, he has been a political leader at the county and state level. Among his many volumes of poetry are *Picture Poems, The Jackknife Horse,* winner of the Roanoke-Chowan Award, and *Spur Line. Journey Proud* amounts to a volume of selected poems. *The Best of Thad Stem, Jr.,* a volume of prose and poetry, was published in 1976.

SHELBY STEPHENSON was born in 1938 on a farm in Johnston County, and many of his poems are rooted in his rural experiences. After graduating from the University of North Carolina and attending law school there, he went on to the University of Wisconsin in Madison, where he earned his Ph.D. He now teaches and heads the Department of English at Campbell College. He is married and has two children. In addition to writing poetry and criticism, Stephenson collects folk, country, and bluegrass songs; he also plays the guitar and sings. One of the state's most prolific poets, he has published his work in many journals, including *Kansas Quarterly, St. Andrews Review,* and *Southern Poetry Review.*

KATHRYN STRIPLING, who grew up in Georgia, has lived for the last decade in North Carolina. She received her M.F.A. from the University of North Carolina at Greensboro, where she studied with Robert Watson and Fred Chappell. She now lives in Webster and teaches at Western Carolina University, where her husband also teaches. Her poems have appeared in over a dozen magazines, including *The American Scholar, Georgia Review,* and *Southern Poetry Review.* She has also been awarded an Academy of American Poets Prize and the Irene Leache Memorial Prize.

JULIE SUK was born in Mobile, Alabama, and attended Stephens College and the University of Alabama. She is married, has three children, and works at the nature museum in Charlotte, North Carolina. Her hobbies include collecting shells, painting, and digging for fossils. Her poems have appeared in a number of poetry journals and anthologies, including *Eleven Charlotte Poets* and *North Carolina Poetry: The Seventies.* Currently she is completing her first book of poems.

CHUCK SULLIVAN was born in New York City but came to North Carolina on a basketball scholarship. He received his B.A. from Belmont Abbey College and his M.F.A. from the University of North Carolina at Greensboro. He began writing while he was a VISTA worker in the mountains of West Virginia. He was basketball coach and English teacher at a Winston-Salem high school but most recently has been working in the Poetry-in-the-Schools Program in South Carolina. He is married and has two children. Among his hobbies he lists sports and theology. His poetry has appeared in such magazines as *Esquire* and *Southern Voices,* and his first book, *Vanishing Species,* was published in 1975.

CHARLEEN SWANSEA was educated at Meredith College and the University of North Carolina at Chapel Hill, where she earned an M.A. The mother of two children, she has been active on the state's literary scene through editing *Red Clay Reader;* founding Red Clay Press, which has brought out a number of works by North Carolina authors; writing poetry; and teaching at Queens College and the University of North Carolina at Charlotte. She has also published a book based on her experience in the Charlotte Poetry-in-the-Schools Program.

THOMAS N. WALTERS was born in Tarboro, North Carolina, and graduated from the University of North Carolina at Chapel Hill with honors in creative writing. He later received his Ed.D. from Duke University. He is married and is an associate professor at North Carolina State University. He has published a number of critical articles on modern poets, a novel for young readers, and two collections of poetry, *Seeing in the Dark,* a book of poems about movies, and *The Loblolly Excalibur and a Crown of Shagbark.* In addition to writing, Walters has been active as a painter and sculptor. One of his hobbies is film-making.

ROBERT WATSON, born in Passaic, New Jersey, has lived in North Carolina for over two decades, no doubt long enough to make him an adopted Tar Heel. He graduated from Williams College in 1946 and holds a Ph.D. from Johns Hopkins. Since 1953 he has been on the faculty of the University of North Carolina at Greensboro, specializing in creative writing and modern fiction. He lives in Greensboro with his wife Elizabeth Rean, an artist, and their two children. Though Watson is an English professor and has published numerous critical articles (he is also a playwright and novelist), he resists being labeled an academic poet. As a rule he avoids literary and mythological allusions, often coloring his poems with a wry wit or rollicking humor. He has written that the main concern of his poetry is "the plight of ordinary men and women."

Watson's work has been widely published in national magazines such as *Poetry, The New Yorker,* and *The Nation.* He has also recorded his poems for the Library of Congress. Following his first collections, including *The Paper Horse, Advantages of Dark,* and *Christmas in Las Vegas,* he published *Selected Poems* in 1974.

MARVIN WEAVER was until recently the director of the Fayetteville Arts Council. He has also taught creative writing at Soul City and been active in the Poetry-in-the-Schools Program in North Carolina. After receiving his M.A. from the University of Alabama, where he edited *The Alabama Review,* he taught at the University of North Carolina at Greensboro from 1968 to 1972. His poems have appeared in many Southern journals, including *The Hollins Critic, Mississippi Review,* and *Greensboro Review.* His first collection, *Hearts and Gizzards,* was published in 1976.

JOHN FOSTER WEST was born in Wilkes County and educated at Mars Hill College and the University of North Carolina at Chapel Hill, where he earned his M.A. in English and was one of the founders of the *Carolina Quarterly.* He has taught at Elon College and Old Dominion University and is now writer-in-residence at Appalachian State University. West has also been active as a folklorist and novelist and has published many science fiction and adventure stories. He is the author of two novels, a nonfiction book on Tom Dula, and two collections of poems, *up ego!* and *Wry Wine.*

JONATHAN WILLIAMS was born in Asheville in 1929 and has spent much of his life on a farm near Highlands. Educated at St. Albans School, Princeton University, and Black Mountain College, he also studied art and design at the Institute of Design in Chicago. In college he became interested in the rebellious and experimental poems that came to be labeled Beat poetry. His early poems were published in *Black Mountain Review.*

Williams, however, has not confined himself to writing experimental poetry; he lists his occupations as "poet, publisher, designer, essayist, iconographer." In 1951 he founded his own publishing company, Jargon Press, and has published such avant-garde writers as Charles Olson, Kenneth Patchen, and Henry Miller, as well as a number of his own experimental books. He has also been active in giving readings and lectures throughout the United States and Europe. Among his hobbies are gardening and long-distance hiking, both of which have influenced his poetry. Drawing on a wide variety of subject matter—jokes, politics, and other topical themes, as well as universal ones—Williams calls himself a "visual poet" and often illustrates his poems with pictures or cartoons. His work shows his awareness of such diverse poets as Walt Whitman, Ezra Pound, Catullus, and Basho. His poetry has been widely published here and abroad, and he has appeared in nearly thirty anthologies. Among his most representative titles are *The Empire Finals at Verona, Amen/Huzza/Selah,* and *Blues & Roots/Rue & Bluets.* His selected poems, *An Ear in Bartram's Tree,* was published in 1969.

EMILY HERRING WILSON was born in West Point, Georgia, and educated in North Carolina, earning her B.A. at the University of North Carolina at Greensboro and her M.A. at Wake Forest University. Married to a Wake Forest professor, she is the mother of three children and has worked as a journalist and teacher. She is currently an instructor at Reynolda House in Winston-Salem. Since studying poetry under Randall Jarrell, she has published widely in regional journals. Her poems have been collected in two books, *Down Zion's Alley* and *Balancing on Stones.* She is one of the founders of the Jackpine Press, which specializes in publishing Southern poetry.

J. S. WINKLER was born in Lenoir, North Carolina. After graduating from Ohio Wesleyan, he was a Fulbright Scholar in Tübingen, later receiving his Ph.D. in Germanic languages and literature from Princeton University. He taught at the University of Mississippi and Winthrop College, and since 1961 has been on the faculty at Davidson College. He is married and has three children. His poems, articles, and translations have appeared in a number of regional journals, and his first book, *The Ghost in the Dog Trot*, was published in 1975. Any reader of his poetry will learn that he is an avid trout fisherman.

Selected Bibliography

Adcock, Betty. *Walking Out*. Baton Rouge: Louisiana State University Press, 1975.

Ammons, A. R. *Collected Poems: 1951–1971*. New York: W. W. Norton & Co., 1972.

———. *Diversifications*. New York: W. W. Norton & Co., 1975.

———. *The Snow Poems*. New York: W. W. Norton & Co., 1977.

———. *Sphere: The Form of a Motion*. New York: W. W. Norton & Co., 1974.

———. *Tape for the Turn of the Year*. Ithaca, N. Y.: Cornell University Press, 1965.

Applewhite, James. *Statues of the Grass*. Athens: University of Georgia Press, 1975.

Barrax, Gerald. *Another Kind of Rain*. Pittsburgh, Pa.: University of Pittsburgh Press, 1970.

Bartels, Susan L. *Step Carefully in Night Grass*. Winston-Salem, N. C.: John F. Blair, Publisher, 1974.

Bayes, Ronald H. *The Casketmaker*. Winston-Salem, N. C.: John F. Blair, Publisher, 1972.

———. *King of August*. Laurinburg, N. C.: The Curveship Press, 1975.

———. *Porpoise*, Charlotte, N. C.: Red Clay Books, 1973.

Beecher, John. *Collected Poems, 1924–1974*. New York: Macmillan, 1974.

Bevington, Helen. *Beautiful, Lofty People*. New York: Harcourt Brace Jovanovich, 1974.

———. *When Found, Make a Verse Of*. New York: Simon and Schuster, 1961.

Brookhouse, Christopher. *Scattered Light*. Chapel Hill: University of North Carolina Press, 1969.

Chappell, Fred. *River*. Baton Rouge: Louisiana State University Press, 1975.

———. *The World Between the Eyes*. Baton Rouge: Louisiana State University Press, 1971.

Deagon, Ann. *Carbon 14*. Amherst: University of Massachusetts Press, 1974.

———. *Poetics South*. Winston-Salem, N. C.: John F. Blair, Publisher, 1974.

———. *There Is No Balm in Birmingham.* Boston: Godine Press, 1977.

Eaton, Charles Edward. *Countermoves.* New York: Abelard-Schuman, 1962.

———. *The Greenhouse in the Garden.* New York: Twayne, 1955.

———. *The Man in the Green Chair.* New York: A. S. Barnes, 1977.

———. *On the Edge of the Knife.* New York: Abelard-Schuman, 1969.

———. *The Shadow of the Swimmer.* New York: Fine Editions Press, 1951.

Fields, Julia. *East of Moonlight.* Charlotte, N. C.: Red Clay Books, 1973.

Grey, Robert Waters, ed. with Charleen Swansea (Whisnant). *Eleven Charlotte Poets.* Charlotte, N. C.: Red Clay Books, 1971.

———, ed. with Nancy Stone. *White Trash: An Anthology of Contemporary Southern Poets.* Charlotte, N. C.: The New South Co., 1977.

Hardison, O. B., Jr. *Pro Musica Antiqua.* Baton Rouge: Louisiana State University Press, 1977.

Harmon, William. *The Intussusception of Miss Mary America.* Santa Cruz, Cal.: Kayak Books, 1976.

———. *Legion: Civic Choruses.* Middletown, Conn.: Wesleyan University Press, 1973.

———. *Treasury Holiday.* Middletown, Conn.: Wesleyan University Press, 1970.

Heffernan, Thomas. *Mobiles.* Laurinburg, N. C.: St. Andrews College Press, 1974.

Hulme, Francis Pledger. *Mountain Measure.* Boone, N. C.: Appalachian Consortium Press, 1975.

Jarrell, Randall. *The Complete Poems.* New York: Farrar Straus, 1969.

———. *The Lost World.* New York: Macmillan, 1965.

———. *Selected Poems.* New York: Atheneum, 1964.

Jeffers, Lance. *Poems.* Detroit, Mich.: Broadside Press, 1974.

———. *When I Know the Power of My Black Hand.* Detroit, Mich.: Broadside Press, 1975.

Keens, William. *Dear Anyone.* Lisbon, Iowa: Penumbra Press, 1977.

Liner, Amon. *Chrome Grass: Poems of Love and Burial.* Chapel Hill, N. C.: Carolina Wren Press, 1976.

———. *Marstower.* Charlotte, N. C.: Red Clay Books, 1972.

Lipsitz, Lou. *Cold Water.* Middletown, Conn.: Wesleyan University Press, 1967.

Macleod, Norman. *The Selected Poems of Norman Macleod*. Boise, Idaho: Ahsata Press, 1975.

Malone, E. T., Jr. *The Tapestry Maker*. Winston-Salem, N. C.: John F. Blair, Publisher, 1972.

Marcus, Adrianne. *The Moon Is a Marrying Eye*. Charlotte, N. C.: Red Clay Books, 1972.

McCurdy, Harold Grier. *The Chastening of Narcissus*. Winston-Salem, N. C.: John F. Blair, Publisher, 1970.

Miller, Heather Ross. *Horse, Horse, Tyger, Tyger*. Charlotte, N. C.: Red Clay Books, 1973.

Miller, Jim Wayne. *Dialogue with a Dead Man*. Athens: University of Georgia Press, 1974.

Morgan, Robert. *Land Diving*. Baton Rouge: Louisiana State University Press, 1976.

———. *Red Owl*. New York: W. W. Norton & Co., 1972.

———. *Zirconia Poems*. Northwood Narrows, N. H.: Lillabulero Press, 1969.

Newman, Paul Baker. *The Cheetah and the Fountain*. Fort Smith, Ark.: South and West, Inc., 1968.

———. *Dust of the Sun*. Fort Smith, Ark.: South and West, Inc., 1969.

———. *The House on the Saco*. Dublin, N. H.: William L. Bauhan, 1977.

———. *The Ladder of Love*. New York: The Smith/Horizon Press, 1970.

———. *Paula*. Georgetown, Cal.: Dragon's Teeth Press, 1975.

Owen, Guy. *The White Stallion and Other Poems*. Winston-Salem, N. C.: John F. Blair, Publisher, 1969.

——— and Mary C. Williams, eds. *New Southern Poets: Selected Poetry from Southern Poetry Review*. Chapel Hill: University of North Carolina Press, 1975.

——— and Mary C. Williams, eds. *North Carolina Poetry: The Seventies*. Raleigh, N. C.: Southern Poetry Review Press, 1975.

——— and Mary C. Williams, eds. *Southern Poetry: The Seventies*. Raleigh, N. C.: Southern Poetry Review Press, 1977.

Ragan, Sam. *To the Water's Edge*. Durham, N. C.: Moore Publishing Co., 1972.

———. *The Tree in the Far Pasture*. Winston-Salem, N. C.: John F. Blair, Publisher, 1964.

Reddy, T. J. *Less Than a Score, But a Point.* New York: Vintage Books, 1974.

Reeves, Campbell. *Bane of Jewels.* Francestown, N. H.: The Golden Quill Press, 1968.

———. *Coming Out Even.* Durham, N. C.: Moore Publishing Co., 1973.

Ruark, Gibbons. *A Program for Survival.* Charlottesville: University Press of Virginia, 1971.

———. *Reeds.* Lubbock: Texas Technology College Press, 1977.

Sauls, Roger. *Light.* Chapel Hill, N. C.: Loom Press, 1974.

Seay, James. *Let Not Your Hart.* Middletown, Conn.: Wesleyan University Press, 1970.

———. *Water Tables.* Middletown, Conn.: Wesleyan University Press, 1974.

Shaw, Sharon. *Auctions.* Winston-Salem, N. C.: John F. Blair, Publisher, 1977.

Sprunt, William. *A Sacrifice of Dogs.* Laurinburg, N. C.: St. Andrews College Press, 1976.

Stem, Thad, Jr. *Journey Proud.* Charlotte, N. C.: McNally and Loftin, 1970.

———. *Penny Whistles and Wild Plums.* Charlotte, N. C.: McNally and Loftin, 1962.

———. *Spur Line.* Charlotte, N. C.: McNally and Loftin, 1966.

Sullivan, Chuck. *Vanishing Species.* Charlotte, N. C.: Red Clay Books, 1975.

Walters, Thomas N. *The Loblolly Excalibur and a Crown of Shagbark.* Raleigh: N. C. Review Press, 1976.

———. *Seeing in the Dark.* Durham, N. C.: Moore Publishing Co., 1972.

Watson, Robert. *Selected Poems.* New York: Atheneum, 1974.

Weaver, Marvin. *Hearts & Gizzards.* Laurinburg, N. C.: The Curveship Press, 1975.

West, John Foster. *Wry Wine.* Winston-Salem, N. C.: John F. Blair, Publisher, 1977.

Williams, Jonathan. *Blues & Roots / Rue & Bluets: A Garland for the Appalachians.* New York: Grossman Publishers, 1970.

———. *An Ear in Bartram's Tree.* Chapel Hill: University of North Carolina Press, 1969.

———. *Elite Elate Poems.* New York: Grossman Publishers, 1974.

————. *The Loco Logodaedalist in Situ.* London: Cape Goliard Press, 1972.

Wilson, Emily Herring. *Balancing on Stones.* Winston-Salem, N. C.: Jackpine Press 1975.

————. *Down Zion's Alley.* Winston-Salem, N. C.: Drummer Press, 1972.

Winkler, J. S. *The Ghost in the Dog Trot.* Chapel Hill, N. C.: Briarpatch Press, 1975.